Classic Thai

Classic Thai

Design · Interiors · Architecture

Photography by Luca Invernizzi Tettoni
Texts by Chami Jotisalikorn, Phuthorn Bhumadhon
and Virginia McKeen Di Crocco

PERIPLUS

Published by
Periplus Editions (HK) Ltd

Copyright © 2002
Periplus Editions (HK) Ltd
Photographs © 2002 Luca
Invernizzi Tettoni

ISBN 962-593-849-4
Printed in Singapore

Editor: Kim Inglis
Associate Editor: Jocelyn Lau
Design: mind, London

Distributed by:
North America
Tuttle Publishing
364 Innovation Drive
North Clarendon
VT 05759–9436
Tel: (802) 773 8930
Fax: (802) 773 6993

Asia Pacific
Berkeley Books Pte Ltd
130 Joo Seng Road #06-01
Singapore 368357
Tel: (65) 6280 3320
Fax: (65) 6280 6290

Japan and Korea
Tuttle Publishing
Yaekari Building, 3F
5-4-12 Ōsaki, Shinagawa-Ku,
Tokyo 141–0032
Tel: (813) 5437 0171
Fax: (813) 5437 0755

Contents

Foreword *by M.R. Sukhumbhand Paribatra*

When one sees a classic Thai object, be it a necklace or a ceramic jar, a manuscript cabinet or a stucco temple motif, the item immediately distinguishes itself as being uniquely Thai. This is in great part due to its decoration, with floral or vegetal designs, the tapering shape and the mastery of craftsmanship, utilizing skills and styles that have been handed down over centuries, if not millennia.

Similarly, when one visits a Thai palace, temple compound or typical classic Thai house, there is no question as to its origin and heritage. Be it the glittering roofs of Bangkok's Grand Palace, the soaring silhouette of a wooden house on stilts, or a towering bell-shaped *chedi* rising from the central plains: they all reflect an unmistakably Thai image.

However, this immediately identifiable 'Thai style' is not a static phenomenon. This book traces its evolution, from its 13th-century Khmer heritage, through centuries of development and adaptation, to the present day. From the ancient capitals of Sukhothai and Ayutthaya, to the northern Lan Na Kingdom and today's Ratanakosin era, the influences from Siam's surrounding neighbours are apparent. Shapes, lines and motifs from India, Sri Lanka, the Mon people, Myanmar (Burma), China and even classical Europe, are now constant features of the Thai architectural landscape. Somehow, the Thais have managed to absorb many different styles, adapt them to their own use, and then re-export them, in their new Thai-style incarnation, oftentimes back to the people from whence they came.

Thai belief in Buddhism and the Thais' veneration of their monarchy are embedded in the arts. Over the centuries, artists, architects and artisans have built countless palaces and temples, to venerate both the Buddha and the King. Similarly, Buddha images have always held pride of place in the monasteries as the centre of the Thai religious universe, and because of the tradition of making merit, such images, along with other temple accoutrements (manuscript cabinets, altars, pulpits, ceremonial containers and so on) have flourished. Similarly, items crafted for wealthy patrons, in the form of jewelry, furniture, ceramics, textiles and more, have played an important role. This publication offers an in-depth analysis of this tradition of design and craftsmanship.

Moreover, recently, it has become popular, amongst both Thais and foreign residents, to try to preserve and emulate this tradition in domestic architecture and interiors. One of the major features of classic Thai architecture is its transportability. Built entirely from wooden panels, domestic houses lend themselves to being dismantled, moved to a new site, and reassembled or rebuilt with adaptation.

It is an increasingly common sight to see such houses in a metropolitan setting, and to witness typical Thai items used in their interior decoration. Whereas once traditional Thai houses would have had reed matting, cushions and perhaps a *tang* (a low square or rectangular seat/table) or two, today they are furnished with vernacular panache. Manuscript cabinets double up as television repositories, sofas are upholstered in Thai silk, and parts of gables may be hung on the walls as decoration. Similarly, banners once reserved for the temple, are displayed as modern-day *objets d'art*. This book showcases a variety of such Thai-style houses adapted for modern-day use.

Opening with a chapter on the classic Thai house, then following through with an in-depth analysis of the country's prime religious and royal sites, and ending with a cornucopia of Thailand's arts and crafts, *Classic Thai* is an inspiring addition to the ongoing analysis of Thai style.

The Classic Thai House

Many would argue that the most enduring icon of Thai style and design is the traditional Thai house. With its raised platform on stilts, triangular shape and steep gabled roof descending from an elongated pinnacle into curved, flame-shaped eaves, this sinuous silhouette rising from a tropical landscape is a sublime image. The structure developed directly from the needs of an agricultural community that had to adapt to a hot, tropical environment subject to seasonal flooding. Rooted in a centuries-old agrarian culture, what is recognized as the classic Thai house today is surprisingly little changed from its original form dating back to the first settlements along the river deltas of old Siam. This tenacity of form can be attributed to the singular principle governing the structure of the Thai house: that form follows function.

Ironically, it was the American architect Louis Henri Sullivan who originated this dictum that went on to inspire a generation of *fin-de-siècle* American and European architects in search of modern forms. In the early 20th century, Sullivan advocated that modern architecture should try to integrate ornamentation into the design of the building itself rather than be applied as mere external decoration. He pioneered a new school in western architecture that broke away from historic trappings and the external ornamentation that marked the buildings of his predecessors. A few decades on, in the mid 20th century, Swiss architect Le Corbusier conceived the notion of the home as a 'machine for living'. His breakthrough recipe for the International Style included, among other features, buildings raised off the ground level on stilts to encourage greater airflow, a free-flowing floor plan, and a roof garden used for social activities — three features that are the defining characteristics of the traditional Thai house.

Thus, if one were to analyse the traditional Thai form within a world view of architectural history, the classic Thai house, though extant for centuries, can be viewed as thoroughly 'modern' in its embodiment of the structural theories dictated by two visionaries of early western modernism. From this perspective, it is ironic that the recent decades of Thai economic boom have resulted in the number of traditional Thai houses dwindling; rapid modernization, diminishing timber resources and a hunger for western forms are the main reasons for its demise. Modern Thais are eager to shake off their past as an agricultural society and embrace cement houses and high-rise living as epitomized by the West.

Thai communities were traditionally located along waterways, thus many houses were either built on stilts or actually floating in the water. The floating houses generally consisted of twin houses that served as both a home and a shop. The living quarters were located in the back, while the open-fronted unit in the front was used as a shop where goods were displayed and sold. These floating houses lined the rivers wherever settlements existed, and could be moved around if needed. These days floating houses have vanished from Bangkok's riverbanks, but can still be found deep in the countryside. Similarly, there are still examples of traditional houses used as residences in the provinces, and some in Bangkok, though the latter are usually preserved as museums and palaces. Less common are Thai-style contemporary residences in Bangkok; the ones that do exist are usually constructed from a number of single-room houses — transported from another province and reassembled in the city to form a large cluster house.

Houses built in this manner embody the key characteristic of a traditional Thai house — namely transportability. Built

Below: The severe, yet elegant lines of this house exemplify the geometric precision that governs the rules of proportion in Thai houses. When well-crafted, the result is a perfection of symmetry and form as seen in this stunning example, a reconstructed house located in Ayutthaya and open to the public.

Right: In contrast to the magnificent scale of the red palace that was built to commemorate King Rama II's birthplace (see opposite), his actual home, shown here, seems modest in comparison. This house was his residence before he ascended the throne, and was later donated to Wat Rakang in Thonburi, for use as a library. In the 1980s it underwent a restoration, with the aid of noted painter Fua Horapitak.

Opposite: The Rama II Memorial House was built as a museum to commemorate the birthplace of King Rama II, an accomplished poet, artist, and patron of Thai classical dance. The most striking aspect of this house is its enormous scale, befitting its status as a memorial to a king. Built as a museum rather than a dwelling, the main building is a cluster house consisting of three large units comprising an antiques gallery, a bedroom gallery, and a sitting room gallery displaying antique Thai decorative objects and furnishings.

entirely of wood, the walls, doors, windows and gables consist of separate wood panels which are fitted together using wooden joints held in place by wooden pegs. No nails are used, thus the entire structure can be taken apart and easily reassembled. The word traditionally used in Thai for house building is *prung*, meaning 'assemble'. Thus the house can be quickly assembled or dismantled and moved from site to site.

Thai houses differ in the north and south, but the style considered to be the classic one is that of the central plains, where Thailand's kingdoms of Ayutthaya, Sukhothai and Bangkok are located and therefore where the Thais reached the height of their culture and power. There are five basic elements of a traditional Thai house: stilts, inward sloping walls, high gables sloping downward into long projecting eaves, a large raised verandah connecting the separate rooms, and extendable rooms. The open space beneath the house serves a number of practical functions, such as providing structural resistance to inclement weather, respite from seasonal flooding, protection from wild animals, ventilation and a shady space to work and store farm tools and the Thai country cart or *kwien*. During the flood season, the space becomes a place to moor boats. In the southern coastal settlements the houses are built on tall stilts, but the stilts become progressively shorter as one travels northwards and into the mountains.

The distinctive inward sloping walls serve a structural function and are a result of the local environment. In order to cope with seasonal floods, the dwellings had to either float or

stand on stilts. Exposure to heavy flooding and strong winds meant that the stilts had to be high and braced, hence the tri-angulated structure. In the central plains, where there is mild inland flooding, the stilts and structural frames slope inwards, giving the house the stability and structural reinforcement it needs. The high gable extends the height of the room for heat convection, while the long projecting eaves protect the house from heavy monsoon rains. The partially-covered *chan-ban* verandah is a huge platform on stilts. It connects the bedroom units and provides a communal living area for the inhabitants. The covered parts are used for day-to-day social activities, and the uncovered space is used for ceremonies, feasts, drying food and growing plants. The house breathes through the spaces in its floors, wall panels and gables and, since the bedrooms are separate units, it can obtain ventilation from any direction.

There are many variations of this classic house style, ranging in size from a single-family house to a cluster house. The smaller house consists only of a bedroom and a kitchen, while the cluster house may have up to five or six bedrooms arranged around the *chan-ban* verandah. In the traditional extended family system in old Siam, additional bedrooms were added as the family size increased; the verandah platform is extendable and some houses became longer as more living units were added on. Traditionally, the groom left his family home to join the bride's family, so often he would remove his room from his parents' house and take it with him to add to his new bride's home.

Due to the complex social system of heirarchy based on age and seniority, rooms are sometimes placed at different heights or levels on the verandah platform. The owner's room is always located in the most important place and usually at the highest level. The levels may vary only slightly, but the distinction represents the social hierarchy of space so characteristic of Thai architecture. From a structural perspective as well, this arrangement also allows breezes to pass underneath the house and through the spaces in the floor levels. The entrance staircase to a Thai house traditionally faces the canal or river, though today with the disappearance of waterway thoroughfares, entrances now usually face the driveway, or may overlook a pond for dramatic effect. Typically the entrance consists of stairways leading up to one or two platform levels, a purely functional feature created to accommodate both low and high floods. These are usually roofed to form a small pavilion, so they can be used for receptions or social gatherings. In poorer homes this entrance is limited to a simple flight of stairs. The orientation of the house is usually lengthwise, in an east-west direction, to avoid the direct rays of the sun and to benefit from the prevailing southerly winds.

As in other Southeast Asian cultures, the Thais traditionally rested, sat and ate on the floor, which was kept meticulously clean, accounting for the custom of removing the shoes when entering a Thai home. Thai houses traditionally contained very little furniture. Instead, the inhabitants used numerous reed mats on the floor for sleeping or sitting. In richer families, the

Opposite, top left: Once crowding the waterways of Bangkok, floating houses are now rare, glimpsed only occasionally in the deep countryside. This one is a typical floating shophouse, consisting of two rooms with the shop located in front and the living quarters in the rear.

Opposite, top right: Almost every Thai house has a spirit house on its property, to house the spirit of the land that protects the home and its occupants. Daily offerings are made in the form of food and flowers.

Left: Chan-ban verandahs in large, well-to-do houses are typically surrounded by a balustrade to provide security for the inhabitants. In the Rama II Memorial house, this balustrade takes the form of a high wall incorporating bars that enable cooling breezes to pass through.

Below: Typically, classic Thai houses are made entirely of wooden panels, in order to facilitate quick dismantling, transporting and rebuilding in another location.

furnishings consisted of low beds and tables with curved Chinese-style legs (*tang*), or a low dressing table. The bedroom sometimes contained a cupboard or chest to store clothes. The typical kitchen contained a charcoal stove and a screened cupboard for storing food and utensils.

Though the Central Plains house is considered the classic Thai house style, the northern Thai house has a distinctive form with three key features that distinguish it from that of the Central Plains. The most visible of these is the V-shaped design called the *kalae* that caps the apex of the roof gable. The exact origins of the *kalae* remain obscure, but the name has been translated as 'glancing crows'. In some houses, the *kalae* is carved in a manner that resembles the wings of a bird in flight. It is also believed by some that the *kalae* symbolizes a pair of buffalo horns. Generally, *kalae* are found only in upper-class houses, and the design may be derived from the ancient practice of placing buffalo horns on top of the roof to indicate the wealth of the inhabitants. *Kalae* carvings range from simple to ornate, and in more prosperous homes, their elaborate renderings can resemble feathers or flickering flames.

Outward sloping walls are the next visible characteristic of northern houses, and the third characteristic is the carved lintel above the owner's bedroom door. Called *ham yon*, which means 'magic testicles' in ancient northern language, the lintel indicates the bedroom's symbolism as the core of the household. The size of the lintel always corresponds to the length of the owner's foot. Before the lintel is carved, the homeowner

must perform a ceremony inviting magical power to enter the lintel, thus ensuring the fertility of the couple. The designs on the lintel are usually floral, geometric or cloud motifs.

Traditionally, house-building was an event accompanied by numerous rites and rituals that involved the participation of the whole community. Astrologers and monks were consulted and various ceremonies performed. Also, Thais believe that if a house is suitable for humans, it is also suitable for the spirits of the land, so every household sets aside a corner in the compound for a spirit house where the guardian spirit is invited to live. Thus through the house, the building rituals and the miniature spirit house, the owner of the traditional Thai house was linked to both his community and the spirits of the land.

Above: Instead of the steep gabled roofs of Central Thai houses, the roofs of northern houses are topped with V-shaped carvings called *kalae*. The origins of this design remain obscure, but there are three main types: the first is an extension of the bargeboards (as here), the second makes use of wider planks of wood which were carved into a triple curve, and the third style is an attachment in the form of an X, rather than an extension.

M.R. Kukrit Pramoj Home

The residence of former Thai Prime Minister M.R. Kukrit Pramoj, though now open to the public as a museum, is notable in that up until 1995 it was the home of a living person and, as such, represented the way of life of upper class Thai society that has all but died out today. The house stands on a 6,700 sq-m (two-acre) site that was once a mango orchard, but now lies in the heart of what has become Bangkok's business and financial district.

The residence is comprised of five separate single-room teak houses from the central plains of Thailand, three of which are over 100 years old, all connected on the raised *chan-ban* verandah, with an open living space underneath. M.R. Kukrit brought these houses from separate locations at different times, and in the tradition of Thai architecture, had them dismantled, transported, and reassembled in their present location. The first house was acquired in 1960 and the house building process took 20 years to reach its present state of perfection. Each of the five single houses that comprises the upper rooms had specific functions: they include an official reception room, a small private sitting room, a family shrine, a library and the bedroom. The ground-floor space was used as the informal living and dining area, and also contains a meeting room.

M.R. Kukrit directed the building layout himself, and lived according to the old Thai way of life, but with some allowances for modern conveniences such as air conditioning, and a fully equipped modern bathroom. These amenities were integrated into the building without interfering with the appearance of

Right: The highlight of the formal reception room is an antique bed that is believed to have belonged to King Rama II. The family liked to believe that this daybed is where Rama II, an accomplished poet, used to compose his masterpieces. Ornately carved display cabinets contain a very rare collection of exquisite puppet heads which are family heirlooms from the period of Rama V's reign.

Above: The table in M.R. Kukrit's library was once used for secret political discussions during his term as Prime Minister. The Thai display cabinet contains manuscripts of old rare books, photographs and notes from royalty, and photos of ancestors. On top of the cabinet is a very rare statue of Biravana, the Hindu demon god of dance, to whom MR Kukrit would pay homage in a grand annual ceremony.

Right: The Buddha room includes a reliquary that contains part of M.R. Kukrit's ashes. Most of the figures in this room were gifts to M.R. Kukrit, who built this room specially to house them.

the classic exterior, so successfully that even the air-conditioned ground floor looks like the open space traditionally found underneath Thai houses. True to Thai form, these rooms were used as gathering and dining places, while the upper rooms were the private living quarters and reception rooms.

As the residence of a prominent member of a princely family, politician, author, patron of the arts and an important public opinion leader, M.R. Kukrit's home was the site of numerous public functions and visits from foreign dignitaries and important figures in politics and society. A large pavilion hall was added in the later years of the owner's life to accommodate the various receptions, banquets, dance performances and religious ceremonies that M.R. Kukrit often hosted. The pavilion is connected to the residence by a formal walled garden, creating the impression of a unified living compound. The garden contains a famed collection of exquisite Thai miniature trees, or *mai dat*, and a miniature mountain, or *kao mor*, as well as a number of rare plants whose cultivation was personally supervised by M.R. Kukrit, a keen amateur botanist.

Above: M.R. Kukrit was a reknowned patron of Thai classical dance. The large pavilion hall displays a fine collection of *khon* masks worn in Thai classical dance drama performances. The soft facial expressions on some of the masks indicate the craftsmanship of a master mask maker from the reign of Rama VI. The masks depicting human faces are very rare; they date from the early Ratanakosin period when all the dancers, even the human characters, wore masks.

Above: The sitting area of
M.R. Kukrit Pramoj's bedroom
has been left untouched
in the way he lived in it during
his lifetime. This is the room
where he relaxed, listened to
the radio, watched television
and held a small nightly feast
with his beloved dogs. To
the right, a set of altar tables
comprise a small personal
shrine for a Buddha figure
where MR Kukrit prayed
every day.

Right: The antechamber of
the bedroom houses typical
19th-century carved furniture,
but the slatted walls are
a departure from the typical
vertical panelling found in
Thai houses.

Left: The Lacquer Pavilion in the garden was rescued from its dilapidated state in a monastery in the countryside and brought to Suan Pakkad Palace where it was restored by Princess Chumbhot in 1958.

Suan Pakkad Palace

Suan Pakkad, or 'Cabbage Garden Palace', was the property of Prince Chumbhot of Nagara Svarga, a grandson of King Chulalongkorn and the eldest son of Prince Paribatra of Nagara Svarga. The palace is located in the grounds of a former commercial vegetable garden, hence the unusual name.

The former princely residence began life in 1952 as a single reception pavilion. Over the years it was extended with the addition of six traditional houses from various locations in central Thailand connected on to the raised *chan-ban* verandah and walkways. Most of the buildings belonged to the Prince's great-great grandfather, who was one of the two Regents during the time of King Mongkut, or Rama IV, in the mid 19th century. The Prince and his wife were avid collectors of Thai artefacts and antiques: during the process of assembling the building, they decided to use it as a showcase for their collection and opened the palace to the public as a museum.

The highlight of the palace complex is the magnificent Lacquer Pavilion in the garden. Formerly located in the Ban Kling monastery between Ayutthaya and Bang Pa-in on the Chao Phraya River, it is believed that, prior to that, it was part of a royal residence in Ayutthaya. The pavilion was discovered by Princess Chumbhot in 1958 and moved to Bangkok, where it was restored to its present glory. In 1959 the prince gave the pavilion to the princess for her 50th birthday, then died of a heart attack later in the same year. Judging from the style of dress depicted in the murals, the pavilion is believed to date from the early 19th century, otherwise known as the Ayutthaya period.

Right: The Lacquer Pavilion originally consisted of two separate buildings, but to save the buildings from dilapidation, the villagers of the town where it was located dismantled both buildings and rebuilt them to form a new building consisting of an inner chamber within an outer chamber. The inner walls are covered with gold-and-black lacquer painting, known as *lai rod nam* in Thai. This art flourished in the Ayutthaya and early Ratanakosin periods and was applied to manuscript cabinets, boxes, doors and other objects. Designs ranged from classical motifs to a variety of religious scenes. Here, the life of the Buddha along with secular scenes of daily life of that period are depicted.

Above: Situated in the front house, an imposing temple *busabok* houses three Buddha images. The figure in the middle is a Hellenistic-influenced Gandhara style Buddha, from Pakistan. The other two figures are Thai. On the left, an altar holds a set of antique swords.

Right top: A palanquin is placed on top of a low table with lion's feet legs. The tiered umbrella is unfurled over the palanquin's occupant and is a symbol of royalty. To the left, an ornately tiered reliquary serves as a lamp and rests on top of a manuscript cabinet.

Right below: A late 18th-century Ratanakosin period cabinet displays an exquisite collection of gold nielloware, which was used only by nobility. On one side sits an antique dressing table, while on the other side and in the foreground, a gold lacquer ceremonial offering vessel sits atop two ornately carved altar tables.

The pavilion originally consisted of two separate buildings, a *hor trai*, or library for containing religious manuscripts, and a *hor khien*, a three-walled pavilion open on one side. The inner walls of both were covered with black-and-gold lacquer murals depicting scenes from the life of the Buddha, along with charming representations of secular daily life of those days. The outer walls were covered with elaborate wooden carvings of flowers and animals. Originally the *hor trai* consisted of an inner room containing bookcases surrounded by a verandah. It was raised on stilts and stood in a pond.

Due to the severe dilapidation of the *hor khien*, the villagers at Ban Kling monastery dismantled both buildings in order to create a new library, the present-day structure which consists of an inner chamber surrounded by a larger outer chamber. The interior walls are completely covered with lacquer depictions of the life of the Buddha. During this process, many of the original works of art were lost because panels were sawn off and the structure reassembled disregarding the chronology of the events depicted in the murals. Some of the panels were cut and parts lost, while some of the beautiful carvings became hidden within the building's structure, thus destroying any semblance of the original appearance of both *hor trai* and *hor khien*. By the time the pavilion was acquired by Prince and Princess Chumbhot the lacquer had deteriorated so badly that some of the panels were completely blank. It is entirely due to Princess Chumbhot's painstaking restoration that many of the exquisite works of art are now visible today.

Left: On the verandah of the main house, gold-and-black lacquer manuscript cabinets depict scenes from the life of the Buddha and the Ramakien. In the foreground are mother-of-pearl offering vessels, used to present food at ceremonies.

Top: A view of the exterior.

Above: Beside the doorway stands a frame used for placing Buddha tablets, traditionally used in temples. A wood carving above the door depicts a stupa flanked by rows of *theppanom* deities in attitudes of worship.

The Bunnag Home

In the early 1960s Khun Tula Bunnag, then an official in the Royal Household Department, started to build a Thai-style house alongside a *klong* in what was then an idyllic rural area of Sukhumvit Road. Comprising four teak houses brought from Ayutthaya province which are now over 100 years old, the houses are arranged in a square connected by a wide, spacious *chan-ban* verandah. Another Thai house on the ground level was a later addition, built for one of the sons.

The Bunnag residence is significant as a rare example of a traditional building that is still lived in as the contemporary home of an aristocratic family. The family of Tula Bunnag are the direct descendants of Chao P'raya Suriyawongse Bunnag, an important figure in Thai history who was the formidable Regent of Siam during the minority of King Chulalongkorn (Rama V).

The upper rooms of the main house are used as bedrooms, and there is also one formal reception room with a Buddha room annex. A skylight opening cut in the middle of the *chan-ban* verandah allows sunlight to shine on to a fish pond in the open-air space used as the living and dining area beneath the *chan-ban* verandah.

In keeping with the classic Thai house layout, the open-air *chan-ban* verandah, lower living area and uncovered outdoor staircases tend to leave the residence exposed to nature's elements. This is wonderful when breezes circulate during hot days, but when a thunder storm breaks out, it is another matter. "People always ask me what we do when it rains," says

Top: A house on ground level was a later addition as the family grew. The decorative panels beneath the windows were carved by Tula Bunnag.

Above: The house as seen from the leafy garden.

Opposite: In the reception room, a carved manuscript cabinet depicts Buddha's flight from the palace. Resting atop a day bed, a mother-of-pearl tray holds a betel nut set and offering bowl crafted by Tula Bunnag. On the wall hangs a photo of two of King Rama V's sons.

Opposite: Above a gold-and-black lacquer manuscript chest, a portrait of the formidable family ancestor, Chao P'raya Suriyawongse Bunnag, looks out over an arrangement of *poom*, the classic ceremonial floral decorations that are meant to resemble a budding lotus. Beneath the window is a bronze sculpture of the same ancestor, along with family photos including one of Khun Tula with the present monarch, and an heirloom sword.

Below: A view into the Buddha room, a classic feature of an upper-class house. The pot on the left is a traditional Mon terracotta water jar.

Right: A type of altar known as *attachan* stands beside a traditional dressing table. In the foreground a mother-of-pearl inlay tray holds a set of antique Bencharong dishes.

Khun Tula's widow Khun Chancham, a writer noted for interpreting the English edition of M.R. Kukrit Pramoj's most famous novel, *The Four Reigns*. "And I always tell them, well everything gets wet, of course."

Reflecting the family's history, the sprawling Bunnag residence is stuffed full with heirlooms of Thai antiquity, decorative wood carvings, delicately crafted mother-of-pearl inlay objects that Khun Tula carved as his hobby, as well as people and animals spilling over each other in the course of everyday life. Exquisite Thai antiquities form the backdrop to the family's daily life, merging into the living space with a casual familiarity derived from a shared history over many generations.

True to tradition, the open-air ground level beneath the *chan-ban* verandah is used as a dining room and sitting area that opens onto the garden, providing easy access for the influx of plants, animals and friends. "An authentic Thai house is supposed to be messy and lived in," chuckles son Khun Tew Bunnag, as a gleaming rooster struts across the dining-room floor, followed by several cocker spaniels. "Daily life creates clutter. This isn't a museum, it's a real Thai home."

Above: Particularly large *chan-ban* verandahs such as this one normally have a central skylight opening to accommodate a shady tree. This one allows sunlight to fall onto a fish pond beneath.

Opposite: A collection of Tula Bunnag's mother-of-pearl creations on display with the *chan-ban* verandah behind.

The Prasart Museum

The Prasart Museum, located on Krungthep Kreetha Road on the outskirts of Bangkok, was built to house owner Prasart Vongsakul's collection of Thai prehistoric artefacts, Buddha images, pottery, Thai furniture, paintings and porcelain. An avid collector who had been amassing objects for 20 years before he started building his museum in 1980, Khun Prasart realised that many of Thailand's most precious *objets d'art* had been taken abroad by foreign collectors. Concerned that the country was losing its artistic heritage, he hoped to preserve these objects in Thailand for the benefit of future generations.

To provide a classical setting for the collection, the museum calls on a variety of buildings, each an example of classical Thai architecture. They include a temple designed by the owner, a teakwood library or *hor kaeow* set on stilts over a pond in the traditional manner, and a Lan Na pavilion, among others.

The highlight of the museum is the Red Palace, modelled after the original Tamnak Daeng now located in Bangkok's National Museum, which was built as a royal residence for a princess during the reign of Rama II. The original palace is 200 years old and upon seeing its dilapidated condition, the owner decided to replicate the building, lest the original fall into ruin. The replica is built to a smaller scale than the original and is made of rare golden teakwood and crafted by artisans from all over Thailand. Some parts, such as the pillars and doors, are antiques sourced from old temples. The building is sectioned into three rooms; a main sitting room, a bedroom, and a smaller room that probably served as a dressing room in the old days.

Right: The main sitting room inside the Red Palace houses mostly Thai objects from the Ayutthaya and early Ratanakosin periods. On the left, a display cabinet on top of a carved Thai table is a rare example of a style of furniture that was used only by royalty. An 18th-century Thai temple carving of the Hindu god Vishnu on top of a garuda is displayed atop a manuscript cabinet in an extraordinary style that is intricately carved in wood and retouched in gold. In the corner is a 19th-century Thai monk's pulpit, used for preaching sermons. To the right is an enormous 19th-century Chinese decorative screen, carved in wood and covered with gold leaf. The standing and reclining Buddha figures, as well as the figure of the seated monk in the foreground are 19th-century Burmese from the Mandalay period. Paintings on window shutters was not a traditional Thai custom, but the painted shutters in the Red Palace are a creative touch added by the owner.

Right: A small concrete-and-marble temple building was designed by the owner. The body is designed in the Ratanakosin style, while the gable is of carved wood and covered with glass mosaic, in the Ayutthaya style.

Far right: Detail of the painted door in the Red Palace depicts a decorative scene of *theppanom*, or celestial beings, in attitudes of worship, gathering together to pray to the Lord Buddha.

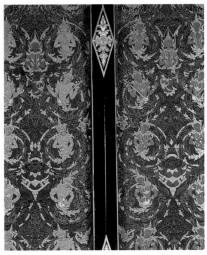

Left: Following the strict rules governing the placement of rooms, the open porch in front of the bedroom shows the unusually high steps rising up to the room, as befits the rank of its royal occupant. In the old days, these steps were removed at night to provide greater security for the princess inside. A collection of mother-of-pearl offering containers is displayed on top of an early 19th-century bed that originally belonged to Rama II. Behind is a black-and-gold lacquer manuscript cabinet. Khun Prasart's team of artists painted the scene in gold leaf on the shutters.

Right: Inside the temple, a 14th-century late Sukhothai period Buddha rests on top of a lotus pedestal and altar carved from teak and covered in gold leaf. Both pedestal and altar were designed by Khun Prasart and crafted by his team of artisans in 1980. The decorative panel hanging from the ceiling shows a classic Thai pattern painted on golden teak. The frame hanging down is made of carved wood covered in gold leaf.

Hua Hin Beach House

Though the Thai-style beach house of M.R. Saisanidh Rangsit is visible to strollers on Hua Hin Beach as an elegant old house set back on an expansive lawn stretching down to the sea, the house originally started out in a much humbler guise, on a different location at the rear of the property. Built 30 years ago by the current owner's father, H.S.H. Prince Sanidh Rangsit, it was originally servants' quarters located behind the main house. The house follows the strict social hierarchy that governs Thai architecture as it is constructed of *mai teng*, or Malaysian hardwood, and *mai yang* or rubber wood. These are fairly common woods and suitable for such edifices (the most precious and rare woods are reserved for royalty and the nobility).

By the time M.R. Saisanidh took over the estate, the old servants' quarters were beginning to subside. He had the option to either let them fall down, or dismantle the various parts to salvage what he could, and reassemble the house. Choosing the latter option, he also decided to relocate the house to another site, and found a spot on the property beside a canal that offered a view of the sea.

"When my father saw the new location he was so pleased," said M.R. Saisanidh, "he said it was the same spot he himself had originally thought to put the house 30 years ago!"

M.R. Saisanidh sketched the new design and layout for what was to become the reassembled house and employed la local craftsman to build it. The craftsman lived on site during the six months it took to complete the job, setting up

Above: View of the house from the lawn overlooking the beach.

Right: The open-fronted porch in front of the master bedroom is comfortably appointed with triangular pillows, a wooden daybed in the foreground and a bamboo bed at the far end, all forms of typical Thai furnishings.

Left: The rooms are placed side by side on an elongated *chan-ban* verandah facing the beachfront, providing ample sea breezes and a full view of the sunrise.

Below: The main sitting and dining area is an open-air section in the front of the *chan-ban* verandah, overlooking the vast lawn spreading down to the beach. A reed floor mat and rattan low-level *khantoke* trays used for serving food are classic country-style furnishings.

Opposite: The master bedroom is dominated by a four-poster bed in the Chinese style that was popular during the reign of Rama II. Silk cushions provide luxurious seating on the floor.

a little camp complete with his family and chickens. "It doesn't take an architect to build a Thai house, if you have a good craftsman," explains M.R. Saisanidh. "Thai houses are built according to very strict rules of proportion. It's all about getting these right and a good craftsman can do that."

The new configuration consists of two rooms placed side by side on top of a long, rectangular *chan-ban* verandah, with the entire house facing the sea. Facing the house towards the waterway is true to Thai tradition, and in this case it fulfills the aesthetic of a beach house as well. For practical purposes, however, the entrance staircase is placed off to the side of the building rather than the front as is customary (in the past one would have arrived at such houses by boat).

The upper rooms are used as bedrooms, with a section of the *chan-ban* verandah roofed and used as the open-air sitting and dining area of the house. The ground section of the house is used as the kitchen quarters.

Right: Exterior view of the house as seen from the lawn facing the waterfront.

Below: The gabled entrance door is typical of large houses of the well-to-do. In such houses, the *chan-ban* verandah is often enclosed within wooden walls or a surrounding balustrade, to provide security for the inhabitants.

A Country Guest House

Though classic Thai houses have become rare in metropolitan Bangkok, the countryside only a few hours' drive from the city offers a landscape of coconut palms, temple spires, gabled houses and a laid-back lifestyle. This country estate belonging to a Bangkok publishing magnate is located on a sprawling riverside property near the old capital of Ayutthaya.

Although the country location of this house would have made it easy to assemble from the numerous old rural houses in the neighbourhood, the owners erected an entirely new house custom built by local craftsmen. This Thai house in fact serves as a guest house, while the family prefers to stay in a large contemporary structure next door.

The Thai house is a large cluster house consisting of three large upper units, each divided into two bedrooms with an open-fronted sitting area in front of each unit. Though the *chan-ban* verandah is extraordinarily large, ample shade comes from a large tree growing through the central skylight. An open-air *sala* that serves as the dining and social area is located to the side of the front entrance door. Kitchen and dining quarters are located on the ground floor. Typically in a Thai dwelling, a small chamber or antechamber in the house is set aside as a Buddha room, but here there is a large single unit house acting as such to the side of the cluster house.

A large open-air *sala* on the river's edge, used for entertaining and dining, is perfectly situated to take advantage of the river breeze and the charming view of an old *chedi* and a Chinese pagoda rising from the opposite bank.

Opposite: Typically, the ground floor beneath the *chan-ban* verandah is used as the dining and living area of the home. This table is ready for a meal of noodles, set with the classic rooster motif bowls that are popularly used in noodle shops and homes all over the country. One of two buffalo heads is seen in this dining area; they add a touch of whimsy to this house in the countryside, where the water buffalo is the backbone of Thai farming.

Above: The open-fronted porch in front of each room is typical of Thai houses, providing a shady area in which to relax. A Bencharong tea set rests atop a carved Chinese side table. The reclining chair is typical of Thai country furniture.

Right: A single unit house beside the larger house is used as the Buddha room. The altar is housed in an ornately carved bed and a Nepalese *thanka* hangs on the right.

Right: A Thai *sala*, or open-air pavilion, is typically placed at the front of the house and used for social gatherings and relaxing. This one, however, was placed adjacent to the gabled main entrance doorway of the *chan-ban* verandah.

Right below: The expansive verandah is covered by the spreading branches of a tree emerging from the central skylight. Building houses around a large tree allows for shade to cover the seating areas below.

Left: The open-air *sala* on the *chan-ban* verandah is a place for dining and socializing. Decorative panels taken from an ox cart along the ceiling depict elephants, a popular image in Thai art and culture.

The Thai House Hotel

The Thai House Hotel, set in the midst of a lush fruit orchard 22 km (12 miles) north of Bangkok, is a contemporary example of a traditional cluster house dwelling built to accommodate a large household. With its lofty gables visible from afar, it is discernible from the building's considerable size and scale that it is a home belonging to a prosperous up-country family.

Made from golden teak, the structure was custom built for the owners in 1990 by 25 craftsmen from Ayutthaya province. The house consists of seven bedrooms divided among three separate houses set on the raised *chan-ban* verandah. Though built as a contemporary home, the owners adhere to the traditional manner of living: beds and seating are placed on the floor, and air conditioning is eschewed in favour of fresh country breezes; high-ceilinged rooms provide enough air circulation for a comfortable night's sleep. The open ground floor is used as a lobby, dining and sitting area. The centuries-old Thai custom of cultivating potted plants in the home is in ample evidence throughout.

The Thai House Hotel is the home of the Fargrajang family, who run the property as a farm-stay guesthouse. It was the dream of the owners, who formerly ran a travel agency specializing in inbound tours catering to Europeans, to build a traditional Thai house where visitors could experience the idyllic lifestyle of rural Thailand. "Thai houses have become rare," says owner Khun Prasan Fargrajang, who grew up in her father's traditional Thai house, which is still located on the property behind the guesthouse, overlooking the canal. "Most

Above and right: Platform landings situated at different levels along the entrance stairways originated purely from the need to accommodate high and low floods during the monsoon. The platforms are usually roofed to form a small pavilion, and were used as a gathering place. They are usually found in the more well-to-do houses, while poorer homes have only a simple flight of stairs.

of them are old and damaged and it's hard to find the artisans who are able to renovate and maintain the exact traditional style. The few complete ones that still exist either belong to the rich élite or have become museums. Neither type offer a place to stay, and few people these days have the opportunity to experience Thai houses as homes any more."

Taking its cue from the cluster house architecture of the extended family, the hotel treats its guests like members of a rural household. Guests can take part in Thai cuisine cooking courses using herbs and vegetables plucked straight from the kitchen garden, or travel on longtail boats through the canal network behind the house to join in the typical activities of a rural community, such as local temple fairs and ordination ceremonies. The boat ride through the canals extends all the way to Bangkok's Grand Palace pier on the Chao Phraya River.

Opposite: Traditionally, all household activities such as sleeping, eating and resting took place on the floor, which was kept meticulously clean, and explains the Thai custom of removing one's shoes when entering a Thai house.

Opposite, below: Thai homes contained very little furniture. In most households, the occupants used mostly reed mats and pillows; here a bedroom is created with the addition of a mattress and dressing table.

Right: The unusually tall height of these house pillars allows the lower sitting area to enjoy more light and provides greater space for breezes to circulate.

The Jim Thompson House

Known to locals simply as 'The House on the Klong', the house of American architect and businessman Jim Thompson epitomizes the heights of elegance that can be attained through a successful marriage of beautiful objects and exquisite taste. Originally stationed in Thailand with the US Office of Strategic Services during World War II, Thompson became a legend for single-handedly reviving the then-dying craft of Thai silk weaving, bringing the product to international fame, and then mysteriously disappearing in the Malaysian jungle in 1967. A great admirer of all things Thai, Thompson built his house in the late 1950s, at a time when it was completely novel for either Thais or westerners to live in a traditional Thai house. He acquired six old houses from various parts of the country and had them reassembled in 1959 in their current location, choosing a site on the *klong*, or canal, opposite the Bangkrua weaving community that produced his silk.

The oldest and largest house, which is now the main sitting room, came from Bangkrua. Dating from 1800, it had been partitioned to house five heirs who owned the house jointly, but now each desired their own abode. Thompson reassembled the house, reversing the walls so that the exterior window carvings could be enjoyed by the occupants within. The windows of the original house were converted to silk-lined niches to display sculptures. A smaller house from Bangkrua became the kitchen wing, and the remaining houses were found near a village called Pak Hai north of Ayutthaya and were transported to Bangkok by barge along the river and canal. Despite his

Right: Jim Thompson had a preference for exotic, lush and untamed foliage, and referred to his garden as 'the jungle', a description that remains apt to this day. This part of the garden was planted more recently in keeping with the style he so liked. A western-style gravel drive leads up to the front door, which is flanked by two Chinese stone lions — in homage to eastern tradition.

Above: A small chamber adjacent to the main sitting room was formerly used as a storeroom, but is now opened to display the fine antique *kalaga*, or Burmese embroidered tapestry, shown here. A Burmese *nat* figure and a collection of Thai Bencharong containers are displayed atop a Chinese altar table.

Left: Designing the house to suit his own lifestyle, Jim Thompson departed from the Thai tradition of placing the entrance stairway on the outside of the house. Instead, he incorporated a two-storey, western-style entrance lobby inside his Thai house, complete with a marble floor and a grand staircase leading to the upper reception and living rooms. The figure in the niche opposite the staircase is a Burmese gong carrier.

Right: The main sitting room, the largest unit in the house, came from the community across the *klong* and was originally the communal home of five brothers who had partitioned it into five units. The silk-lined niches containing Burmese figures were windows in the original house. The carved Thai table displays a fine collection of antique Bencharong ware, while a lacquer manuscript chest serves as a side table next to the sofa upholstered in Jim Thompson silk.

Opposite: The dining table is made from two antique mahjong tables joined to form one unit. The table is set with 17th-century blue-and-white Chinese porcelain.

Right: Thompson's study contains a stunning limestone Thai Buddha image from the 8th century, or early Dvaravati period. The desk displays an Ayutthaya period sandstone bas-relief carving of Buddha preaching a sermon, along with a collection of 15th-century glazed ceramics from Sawankhalok, near the ancient capital Sukhothai.

Right below: In the master bedroom, an altar table inlaid with mother-of-pearl displays an 11th-century sandstone figure of the Hindu deity Uma that dates from the Lopburi period.

training as an architect, neither Thompson nor anyone in Bangkok at that time knew how to repair or reassemble traditional houses, so workmen were brought in from Ayutthaya, where the craft still existed. Other parts of the house that originated from Ayutthaya are the 17th-century bricks that make up the terrace and the green Chinese tiles that form the parapet.

Although he observed the rituals of house building including the installation of a spirit house on the grounds, Thompson departed from the traditional cluster house layout and placed the houses in a form suited to his personal style. Instead of standing separately on the *chan-ban* verandah, the various houses that comprise the rooms were connected to form one large, contiguous unit. The main residence remains elevated, but replacing the traditional outdoor entrance stairway is a staircase enclosed in a vestibule as in a western house.

A Weekend Retreat

The weekend house of Bangkok public relations lady, Khun Pornsri Luphaiboon, embodies the key feature of a Thai house — transportability. Located in the outskirts of Bangkok, what is now a family country house was once famed as the former home of antiques dealer and socialite Connie Mangskau. In 1961, Connie's friend Jim Thompson persuaded her to build a Thai house just as he had done. He helped her find four old Thai houses from Ayutthaya, then planned the layout himself at the house's original location in Sukhumvit Soi 4. The house was filled to capacity with Connie's impressive collection of Asian antiques and was famed as a place where she entertained such glamorous guests as Jackie Kennedy, Roger Moore, and other international celebrities. By the time the house passed on to Connie's heirs in 1990, the original location in Sukhumvit had become a congested commerical district, surrounded by highrises. Offers to buy the house poured in from people who had known the famous hostess, even from as far as the US and Singapore, but the heirs wished the house to remain in its own country.

Finally, the house was sold to Khun Pornsri Luphaiboon who had known Connie and who intended to keep the house in Thailand. "I bought Connie's house to give it a new life and to keep it in the country," says Khun Pornsri. "The workers who reassembled the house were recruited from Ayutthaya and I think Connie would have liked to know that the descendants of the original builders brought new life back to her old Thai house."

Above: A lotus pond and wooden walkway were specially created at the entrance of the house, to evoke a classic landscape.

Right: A carved temple pediment and antique wooden figurines are the focal points of the main sitting room. The manuscript tablets to the right are Burmese. The Thai silk upholstery fabric is an original Jim Thompson pattern dating from Connie Mangksau's era.

With the help of her sons — an engineer, an architect, and a landscape architect — the new owner had the building dismantled and reassembled at its current location overlooking a small lake in a rural setting outside Bangkok. The original linear layout of the house was re-configured in the classic Thai manner, on a square *chan-ban* verandah with the rooms surrounding a central skylight opening. To complete the traditional setting, a lotus pond was created on the property at the main entrance; it is bridged by a long wooden walkway leading up to the house.

The three upper rooms are used as a main sitting room flanked by two bedrooms. A unique feature of the rooms are the door panels in the configuration of shutters; when closed they form walls, and when opened, they allow for open-air access to the *chan-ban* verandah, ideal for catching cooling breezes on balmy days. The ground level is less traditional, sectioned into additional air-conditioned rooms used for dining and family living.

Opposite: Sliding shutter-style doors allow the room to open out onto the *chan-ban* verandah and catch cooling breezes from the lake. A bamboo floor mat and Mon terracotta water vessels are typically Thai.

Above: In the master bedroom, the louvres inset in the floor-to-ceiling doors are a classic form of panelling in traditional Thai architecture.

A Burmese Thai Hybrid

The Thai house of German businessman Gunther Glauninger was built in 1988 on a piece of land that originally consisted mostly of water. An avid art collector and connoisseur, Mr Glauninger had long admired the highly stylized roofs and complex craftsmanship of Thai houses. He also recognized that in the lofty ceilings and open floor plan, the Thai house was suitable for a hot climate. He thought that a Thai-style house would be an inexpensive and efficient way to survive in the tropics, as he would be surrounded by tall leafy trees on the water.

With the help of an architect, the house layout was designed to take advantage of the prevailing southerly winds. The drawing room unit has shuttered walls that open out onto the pond on one side and the garden on the other, to allow the breeze to pass directly through the house, thus making air-conditioning unnecessary.

The house consists of three smaller house units combined to form a large cluster house, but the layout is atypical in that the room units are built on different levels connected by stairs and walkways, rather than placed flat on one single *chan-ban* platform as is the norm. This was done to provide a sense of active, moving space, as well as to allow the house to flow around a central garden.

Entirely custom designed, the building was made by five craftsmen from Ayutthaya and took two years to build. Though relatively new, the house made use of old wood, giving it the rustic, charming appearance of an older residence.

Above: The roofed entrance gate to the house is made from Ratanakosin period Thai temple doors, depicting temple guardian figures carved in bas relief. On either side stand two nearly life-size 19th-century Burmese figures, typically used as gong holders.

Opposite: A Burmese gong circle taken from a classical orchestra functions as a coffee table. A carved triangular gable from a northern Thai *sala* hangs above a fine piece of temple balcony panel from Burma. On the shelf above the window are a row of Thai coconut scrapers called *kratao khod maprao*, or 'grating rabbits'.

Above: On the verandah outside a bedroom, two Mon wooden figures of monks stand one on each side of the doorway. The carved wooden eave bracket supporting the roof is a Lan Na temple bracket. Beside the desk is a northern Thai fish container made of red lacquer.

Above: Walls with large shutters in the drawing room were designed to allow a cooling breeze from the pond to pass through the house. An illustrated Thai manuscript hangs on the wall behind a 19th-century alabaster Mandalay Buddha; *ca* early 20th century. On one of the house pillars is a fine 19th-century Burmese temple carving.

Left: This garden *sala* was custom built to accommodate the marvellous carved temple gable depicting a *theppanom* diety in an attitude of worship. The panel is double sided so the same image is seen on the reverse side.

Opposite: The highlight of the master bedroom is a Lan Na temple door used as a headboard for the bed. It depicts *theppanom* deities. Displayed on top of the Thai gold-and-black lacquer manuscript cabinet are a collection of Burmese red lacquer containers and an antique Burmese gold lacquer fan used by monks in religious ceremonies.

Left: The antechamber of this bedroom is used as a study and Buddha room; it houses a 19th-century Ratanakosin altar and a gold-and-black lacquer manuscript cabinet. Hanging above the door is a whimsical mirror, probably from a Chinese shophouse, depicting a very early photo of the Thai King and Queen.

Right: A landing stage at the ornately decorated front stairway and a walled enclosure surrounding the upper verandah are classic signals that this is the home of a well-to-do family.

A Northern Ayutthayan Home

The elegant Thai-style residence and meticulously designed garden of this Bangkok property provide an apt setting as a home for Mr Richard Engelhardt, UNESCO Regional Advisor for Culture in Asia and the Pacific. Mr Engelhardt found this property through its owners, Kasidis and Lalita Rochanakorn, his colleagues at the United Nations. The house was assembled by the owners in 1992, with the help of architect Krisada Rochanakorn, the owner's brother.

The rooms on the upper *chan-ban* verandah are constructed from old houses from northern Ayutthaya, and the basic layout is executed in the traditional Ayutthaya style; the rooms are placed around a central skylight opening from which a tall Indian Cork tree provides shade as well as a dainty carpet of delicate white flowers. The three upper rooms consist of the master bedroom, a formal dining room and a casual open-air dining room overlooking the garden. The main living areas are concentrated on the bricked and air-conditioned ground level and comprise sitting rooms, a study and additional bedrooms.

Though architecturally adhering to traditional forms, the house has in fact been cleverly adapted to suit a contemporary lifestyle. Whereas in the purely classical form the bedroom is fronted by an open-air porch used as a sitting area, here what would be the porch area is enclosed to form an antechamber serving as a sitting room outside the master bedroom. Access between the upper and ground floors is created via the use of an inside stairway within this antechamber, thus conveniently replacing the customary outdoor stairway configuration.

Right: A formal dining room located on the upper *chan-ban* verandah, such as this one, is rare, as traditionally the dining area is located on the lower ground level. The two paintings are part of a set of ceremonial spirit paintings from the Yao (Hmien) hilltribe in northern Laos. These are hung in the dining room because the Yao traditionally use these paintings on special occasions, such as Yao New Year. Atop two antique Thai display cabinets containing collections of Thai ceramics are two *khon* masks given as gifts to Mr Engelhardt from the Thai dance grand master with whom he studied as a teenager. Atop the table are reproduction Sukhothai period ceramics.

Right: This antechamber of the master bedroom serves as a cosy upstairs sitting room. The painting on the right is an exquisite contemporary piece executed in traditional style, with traditional materials, depicting the Churning of the Milk Ocean by the gods and demons of the beginning of time, in order to obtain the elixir of immortality. The artist is the winner of a UNESCO – AHPADA Seal of Excellence in Handicraft Products. Below is an antique Thai dressing table. Its short height indicates that it dates from a time when Thai people still sat, ate, and slept on the floor.

Another departure from custom is the use of the upper rooms as dining rooms; dramatic entertaining settings take advantage of the handsome teak panelled walls in the formal dining room and the exotic garden view in the casual dining room. This takes the form of an open air *sala* situated to the side of the front entrance. Laden with cultural symbolism, the garden layout was conceived by Mr Engelhardt and designed by renowned Thai floral designer Sakul Intakul. Based on elements of Ayutthaya period garden design, it is filled with native Thai plants that flourished in gardens of the Ayutthaya period.

Despite the classical nature of the house, a key feature that is absent is the traditional spirit house found in almost every Thai home. This is explained by the house's location in the Pattanakan area of Bangkok. Centuries ago, this land was originally outside the 'sacred' boundary of the city, and was therefore used for burials and thought to be populated by ghosts. The period of King Rama V, or King Chulalongkorn, was the era of modernisation in Thailand, when western styles and customs were introduced and adopted, among them the idea that belief in ghosts was superstitious. As this area was Crown Land, and was set aside by the king as a settlement area for Moslems and Chinese Christians, who needed land for the burial of their dead, the houses here do not have traditional spirit houses. Instead, each house, including this one, pays homage to the spirit of King Chulalongkorn, and displays pictures of him as the guardian protector of the land, the houses and their inhabitants.

A Farmhouse in the Metropolis

The guest house of Manuela and Teddy Spha Palasthira is a 100-year-old farmhouse that was brought to Bangkok from Pichit province in central Thailand 30 years ago. An admirer of Thai houses, Khun Teddy had decided to put one in his garden as a pleasant reminder of the idyllic countryside, little envisioning what a megapolis the city would eventually become.

The single unit farmhouse is maintained in its original condition on its original stilts, and is thus very low in height. The ground level is kept open and vacant while the upper level is used as the living quarters, with the inner room used as a bedroom, and the outer porch a sitting area. A single flight of stairs leading up to this outer porch provides the front entrance. Some minor concessions to contemporary comfort were made; an interior flight of stairs was added to allow for access to the modern bathroom that was built in on the ground level.

In 1997 the swimming pool and large *sala* were added, both designed by the owners' daughter, architect Malina Palasthira. Despite its 15m x 4m (50ft x 12ft) dimensions, the pool was designed to give the illusion of greater width via the outward curve along its length. A smaller, glassed and air-conditioned room at one end of the *sala* provides cool comfort on hot or rainy days. Two unique features are evident in this room; the walls consist of single panes of plate glass, custom-made to provide a perfect view of the garden, and the teakwood floorboards are made from single lengths of wood, each extending from one end of the room to the other to provide a smooth, seamless length of teak floor panelling.

Above: An ornately carved antique door frame leads to the pool area. The sizeable open-air *sala* and adjoining swimming pool were designed together specifically for entertaining the numerous guests invited here. The pool is paved in sandstone, which absorbs water, thus keeping bare feet cool.

Right: This century-old house adjacent the pool remains in its original form. The short height and simple, almost crude flight of stairs reflect its origin as a humble farmer's abode. This is an example of a single unit house, with the living quarters upstairs and the open ground level where animals and farm implements were kept.

Far left: Guests sleep on an enormous bed that was originally an antique Thai daybed. Because the bed is wider than the doors and windows, it had to be lifted in through the roof.

Left: Thai houses are typically very dark inside, thanks to dark woods and narrow windows. An antique lamp provides enough illumination for the ornately framed mirror displayed on this desk.

Above: True to traditional form, the front porch of this single unit house serves as the sitting room area. A carving of a garuda hangs on the wall while figures of two Burmese disciples are displayed on a typical Thai daybed. To the left is an antique altar for holding Buddha tablets.

Beung Naiphol

Created by a once-powerful police general as a fantasy residence during the height of Thailand's economic boom, this extravagant lakeside estate on the outskirts of Bangkok was originally named Beung Naiphol, or 'General's House' in Thai. When the economy took a nosedive in the late 1990s, the general's fortunes likewise took a downward spiral and the property was in danger of becoming another real estate casualty, crippled by its enormous size and shrivelled funds.

In 2000, however, the estate was bought by American financier Gene Davis, who saw the property as an ideal weekend retreat. He hired interior designer Prinda Puranananda of the Bangkok design firm Cowperthwaite & Puranananda to renovate the house in keeping with the building's traditional style while adding elements of modern comfort and luxury.

Custom built by craftsmen from Ayutthaya, there is a main building set on an expansive, tree-filled lawn sloping down to a lake, and an adjacent building located on the waterfront. Built as two separate cluster houses, they share in common an enormously lofty open-air *sala* that is used as a main sitting area, overlooking the swimming pool and the lake.

Five steeply gabled roofs indicate the five upper rooms of the main house. In addition, there is a sixth gabled roof, which is, in fact, the top of the *porte-cochère* at the front drive of the residence. This has been rendered as an elongated and heightened *sala* pavilion, with the classic gabled roof designed at an unusual height and proportion to allow it to blend in with the silhouette of the main house. Since the formal entrance

Above: A view of the house from the driveway. The *porte-cochère* takes the form of an elongated and heightened *sala* pavilion topped with the classic gabled roof, allowing it to blend in with the silhouette of the main house.

Right: The sitting room of the lakeside house has shuttered walls on all sides that open fully to provide a view of the water while catching breezes from all directions. This sitting room set is made of woven water hyacinth. An aquatic plant that tends to clog the Thai rivers and canals with its thick growth, the dried water hyacinth has recently become popular as a durable and inexpensive material for home decor items, handbags and furniture, as seen here.

Right: The open-fronted porch in front of the master bedroom provides a breezy sitting area. These carved Chinese chairs are more comfortable than they look, especially with silk-covered cushions.

Below: An armchair and side table made of woven water hyacinth sit beside an ornately carved balustrade, a typical Thai design commonly seen in old houses.

to the house is a platformed, open-air staircase facing the water according to Thai custom, the *porte-cochère* is located in what is architecturally the back of the house (though it faces the main entrance gate and driveway as in a western-style house). Thus, in architectural terms, the house is designed according to the traditional Thai model, but it skilfully incorporates functional western elements without sacrifice to the overall form.

As is customary, the huge upper *chan-ban* platform has a skylight opening to accommodate a large tree growing in the middle that provides shade to the house's upper level. The upper *chan-ban* platform consists of three large units used as bedroom suites surrounding the central skylight. The large, open-air *sala* used for casual social gatherings is placed at the gabled entrance gate facing the water, and two smaller units flanking the back of the house are used as library rooms.

In the traditional manner, the ground floor is used as the main living, dining and kitchen areas. However, in deference to modern-day comfort and the wishes of the new owner, these rooms are now enclosed in glass and air-conditioned.

Above: An unusual feature of this house are shutter-like doors connecting the rooms on the *chan-ban* verandah. When closed, they form a wall that encloses the rooms in a private inner courtyard. When open, as here, they allow easy access to the outside stairways and for breezes to pass through.

Above: Small Thai lacquer containers provide storage for knick-knacks atop the antique Chinese desk and chair in the study. On the left is a Burmese figure kneeling in an attitude of devotion. The painting above the desk is a Korean antique, while the silk rug is Persian.

Right above: The master bathroom is fully appointed in Thai style. Mirrored panelling incorporated into the closet doors adds an illusion of depth. The wooden dressing table is a Chinese antique. A Bencharong jar and typical Thai blue-and-white porcelain ware make decorative containers for toiletries.

Right: Glazed ceramics are a centuries-old Thai traditional craft. The tiles on the bathtub and floor are designed and laid to echo the pattern of the wood panelling on the walls.

Above: Custom-made upholstery from Jim Thompson Thai Silk Co and a silk Persian rug add luxurious elements to the master bedroom. A silk runner in a Thai ethnic weave adorns the bed. Beneath the window is an ornately carved wooden chest from Afghanistan.

Above: An open-air *sala* looks onto the swimming pool which overlooks the lake.

Left: In a modern take on traditional custom, the open-air *sala*, typically used in Thai houses as a setting for social gatherings, has been rendered here to an enormous scale, and is used as a main sitting room. The furnishings are upholstered in Thai silks and cottons.

A House with a History

Located in the suburban Chaengwattana area of Bangkok, the extensive Thai house complex built by German businessman Karl Morsbach consists of two large Thai-style houses set in large tropical gardens overflowing with lush heliconia plants. A long-time resident of Thailand, the owner had initially lived in a small Thai house in the Sukhumvit area upon his arrival in the country. Drawing upon this experience, he decided to design and build his own Thai house, wanting it to be aesthetically pleasing while adapted to accommodate the practical comforts of a European home.

The current two-house complex originally started off with one very large house. Completed in 1985, the planning of this house took two years, while the construction took one year. In anticipation of building, the owners had combed the countryside well in advance, collecting old wood, doors, window frames, banisters, and other architectural remnants from dismantled old Thai houses. Conceived by the owner and designed with the help of an architect, the house is a successful merge of Thai and European architecture, with the living areas rendered in Thai style and the bedrooms furnished in western style.

The Thai style section of the house is comprised of three separate units on an enormous *chan-ban* verandah, serving as sitting rooms, dining room, kitchen and guest rooms. Two old houses, each 130 years old, were brought from Angthong, near Ayutthaya. These two houses make up the dining room and the guest house, which is a separate annex connected to the main

Above: Traditionally, Thai houses overlooked a river or canal, and the inhabitants would simply descend the steps in front of the house to take their daily baths. In modern times the classic waterway has been replaced by the more convenient swimming pool, as seen here.

Right: Thai rooms are normally dark and narrow. Here the owner broke away from the rigid rules governing the proportion of Thai houses and made the main sitting room wider, with bigger and wider doors and windows to allow more light to enter the room. Wood panels in the walls were replaced with glass panes for the same purpose. A very fine Ayutthaya period black-and-gold lacquer manuscript cabinet stands in the left corner. The collections of red lacquerware grouped around the room are Burmese.

Above: The master bedroom of the second house is a 130-year-old teak house brought from Ayutthaya. It is furnished with Chinese antiques. An intricately patterned blue-and-white textile runner woven by Thailand's northern Meo hilltribe adds an ethnic Thai touch to the bedframe.

Right: The open-air porch outside the bedroom was traditionally used as a sitting area for the room's occupants. In this house, the porch ceiling is 1m (3ft) higher than the standard proportion, so that tall Europeans would not have to stoop. Thus changes in proportion and height were one of the ways the owner adapted his Thai houses to suit a European lifestyle.

house by a wooden walkway. According to the owner's concept, the cavernous main sitting room was custom made to proportions that are bigger and wider than the standard Thai house. Classical Thai houses are normally built with the average dimensions 8m x 3m (25ft x 10ft). The sitting room was designed to be closer to a square shape, with higher ceilings and extremely wide doors. Another departure from classical design was the use of bigger windows and glass planes replacing some of the wood panelling in the walls, thus allowing more light into the rooms.

The owner had learned that sleeping in an old-fashioned Thai house comes with some discomfort, so the bedrooms in this house were designed in the brick western style and fully air-conditioned. The problem of how to unify the wooden Thai buildings and the brick western building into one seamless unit was solved by creating a large entrance lobby in the style of an open air *sala*, topped with a Thai roof, thus providing a central space, or hub, to anchor the disparate architectural elements.

Left: A casual dining nook is located on an open-air corner of the verandah between the kitchen and the main sitting rooms, providing a cosy setting for al fresco casual meals overlooking the lush gardens. What appears to be an open porch of the adjacent room is in fact a wall made of doors cum shutters typically found in Thai houses. At this time the shutters are pulled open to allow for maximum sunlight and airflow. The coffee table and vases are made of typical Thai green celadon.

Opposite, top: One of the numerous sitting areas that are scattered around the upper *chan-ban* verandah of the main house. This cosy corner is located in the central entrance lobby, which is open-air and makes use of glassed skylights and glass paned eaves to allow plenty of sunlight to enter the house. A reproduction Khmer head appears to repose in peaceful slumber against one of the many Thai-style triangular pillows that dot the sitting area.

Opposite, below: In this family sitting corner, the shutters/walls are pulled back to create the sense of an open-air porch used for relaxing activities. During the planning stage of this house, the owners scoured the countryside for decorative elements such as the antique balustrades, coloured glass panels and light fixtures seen here. Typical of old-fashioned Thai houses, these items were bought from dealers who specialize in pieces from old dismantled houses.

Located adjacent to the first house, the second house was built at the request of a German friend who saw the first house and was charmed by the idea of living in a classical Thai-style house. Completed in 1990, the second house is similar in concept to the first in that it is a mix of Thai and European.

In this house, the ground level is designed along western lines, with kitchen, dining and living areas built in brick and air-conditioned. The upper level is executed in classic Thai style, with separate rooms connected on a *chan-ban* verandah and an outdoor *sala*. It consists of two bedrooms and a bathroom. Two large old houses from Angthong, each 130 years old, comprise the bedrooms, while a separate unit was custom built as a bathroom. Located on the front of the upper *chan-ban* verandah is an open-air *sala* containing a sitting area, which is used for casual entertaining such as sunset drinks. The front of this house looks onto a large, lotus pond that was created to fashion a classical setting as well as provide a low-maintenance landscape.

Classic Thai Royal & Religious Architecture

Temple and palace architecture is very different to domestic architecture in Thailand. Since the 17th century during the Ayutthaya period, travellers have expressed surprise at the vast gap between the two. In journals, commentaries and letters, such travellers described the houses of common people as very simple. The houses were built on piles, the walls were made of bamboo and the roofs were of thatch. In contrast, temples and palaces were brick constructions with stucco, gilding and other decoration. Some of the royal pavilions were roofed with tin tiles. Temple and palace buildings were so elaborate that they were absolutely incomparable with commoners' houses.

This phenomenon can be explained by religious, cultural and social reasons: Because of the strong belief in Buddhism, immense wealth and effort was invested in the construction of religious buildings. Furthermore, the country's social organization dictated that the ruled had to provide labour for the king and for public works; hence, much religious, palace and civic construction was provided by the general populace. In fact, more temples were erected than palaces because, by royal tradition, the king, who was the greatest patron of Buddhism, always constructed a special temple for each reign. And the elite and bourgeoisie had to prove their status by donating money for the construction of new temples.

For Buddhists, constructing a new temple results in the continuity of Buddhism, so those who either pay for a new temple, or work on building one, earn merit. Each temple has to have two areas — the sacred or public area (*Buddhavasa*) and the living quarters of the monks (*sanghavasa*). The plan of the sanctuary has to reflect Buddhist cosmology: There is a stupa in the middle representing Mount Sumeru, and normally, the *viharn* (preaching hall) and *ubosot* (ordination hall) and a scripture library are also situated in the sanctuary area. Some temple compounds have a cloister surrounding this area to mark off the sacred area. The area comprising the monk's quarters usually consists of a group of simple, less decorated dwellings.

Palace architecture was no less formulaic. The king was considered to be not only a ruler but also a supremely holy person, an incarnation of the Hindu god Vishnu or Indra, the god who protects Buddhism. As a result, palaces of the God-King had to reflect the ethos of heavenly architecture. The style of such buildings and the elements with which they were decorated are of a special type reserved only for use in palaces and temples. Such elements included multi-storied roofs, gables depicting gods, for example Vishnu mounted on Garuda or Indra mounted on Airavanta, gilding and other decorative detail.

Buddhism and Hinduism have played a significant role in Thailand since the 6th century. Many sanctuaries dating to the early historical period with Hindu and Buddhist images have been found in settlements around the gulf of Thailand, at Ku Bua, U-Thong, Nakhorn Pathom, Lopburi, Chansen, Sri-thep and Khok Peeb. Up until the 14th century, Hinayana Buddhism seems to have been the dominant religion in many Thai states. This was probably because of the close contact between the Thai states and Sri Lanka and the Mon country where Hinayana Buddhism flourished. Furthermore, Hinayana Buddhism, with its tenets of freedom, piety and the simple life, may have been in harmony with the Thai mentality. As Hinayana Buddhism became more important, many states which accepted this sect — for example Sri Lanka, the Mon country, Lan Na, Cambodia, Laos and Pagan — communicated and interacted. This resulted in the exchange of knowledge and artistic practice.

Excavations of 6th–7th-century early religious architecture at U-Thong and Ku Bua have revealed brick stupas of many different shapes. These include square, multi-storied stupas, bell-shaped stupas and the type known as *vihara-stupa* where the stupa sits over a square cell enshrining an image. A base of a rectangular *viharn* with a roof of terracotta tiles was also discovered, as were terracotta false windows dating to the 6th century at U-Thong. They probably decorated a multi-storied roof. A good example of Thailand's oldest extant Buddhist architecture is the 6th-century stupa at Chulaprathon, Nakorn Pathom. Made of bricks, its surface is covered with stucco, terracotta and stucco reliefs depicting mythical animals, plants, Buddha images and the Jatakas (stories of the 547 lives of the Buddha prior to his being born as Prince Siddhartha). Many motifs are similar to the 6th-century Gupta art of the Ajanta caves in India. Hindu images from the 6th century of the Linga, Vishnu and Ganesh, probably enshrined in square brick buildings with multi-storied roofs have also been discovered in Thailand.

The evolution of religious architecture in Thailand is tied to influences from outside its borders. Initially, Indian influence was paramount, then close contact with Pagan, Cambodia, the Mon country and Sri Lanka inspired Thai artists to adapt some of their styles and motifs. This is illustrated by the buildings of the Sukhothai, Lan Na and Ayutthaya Kingdoms of the 14th and 15th centuries. This practice continued even later when Indo-Persian, Chinese and Western art and architecture from the 16th to 19th centuries influenced the Thai tradition.

Left: Ku or repositories for cinerary ashes of members of the Chiang Mai royal family in a corner of Wat Suan Dork, Chiang Mai. Most of these small edifices are not more than 100 years old. They imitate the style of the Lan Na stupa, but have lower tower structures.

Opposite, top: Stupa with recessed corners on a triple square base at Wat Phu Khaothong, Ayutthaya. According to the chronicles, King Bayinnaung of Burma erected it in 1569 to commemorate his victory over Ayutthaya. In 1744, King Boromkot of Ayutthaya renovated it so that it now reflects the style of late Ayutthaya on the top with a mix of Pegu architecture reflected in the base.

From the middle of the 15th century onwards, two kinds of Buddhist monasteries were built in Sukhothai and Lan Na: those in the town and those in the forest. The latter type might have been used by monks who practiced meditation, but, regardless of their function, almost all contained a stupa. The stupa was constructed to enshrine the Buddha's relics and was also a memorial structure commemorating the Nirvana of the Buddha.

The most popular shape for the early Thai stupa was the bell, but regional variations emerged over time. There was the *prang* shape at Ayutthaya, the lotus shape at Sukhothai and the bell shape over high square base at Lan Na. Some styles of stupa were popular during a certain period, then fell out of favour, only to re-emerge later. For instance, the bell-shaped stupa was very popular in the 15th–16th-century architecture at Sukhothai and Ayutthaya, but it was replaced by the *prang* shape and the recessed bell shape in the 16th and 17th centuries. In the mid 19th century, however, the bell-shaped stupa was seen again; Rama IV reintroduced it as it was a form he found

particularly pleasing. Within these different categories of stupa, there were also various stages of development. For instance the stocky *prang* shape of the early period developed into the thin, tall *prang*, and the bell-shaped stupa developed recessed corners over time. Most stupas were made of brick or laterite and were coated with stucco. Some were hollow in order to enshrine a Buddha image or miniature stupa.

The *ubosot* and *viharn* were similar structures, rectangular in plan. In the early period, they were open-pillared halls and some such from the Lan Na Kingdom are still extant. Later on, walls with slits for air and light were built. It is thought that windows were introduced in the Ayutthaya period, in the 16th and 17th centuries. Stucco decoration on the frames of windows and doors in high relief took many shapes — *prasat* (tower), crown and others. The inner walls were sometimes painted with murals of the Buddha's life, tales of the Jataka and literature aimed at educating visitors on both Buddhist tenets and secular matters. Boundary stones (*bai sema*) were placed around the

Below left: The 72-m-high (230ft) stupa of bell shape at Wat Yai Chaimongkon, Ayutthaya is the main structure of the temple. Historical sources mention that King Naraesuan erected the stupa in this temple to commemorate his victory over the Burmese army in 1593. This is the popular belief, but some Thai art historians suggest that it has a hollow structure which was probably influenced by Persian designs in the 17th century. The bell part of the stupa is situated on several square and octagonal bases. There are four small stupas surrounding the main edifice which probably indicate the five Buddhas of our world-aeon (*kappa*) in Hinayana Buddhist theology. Sometimes the Buddhist faithful worship this stupa by robing it in a yellow cloth.

Below right: Mural of Phra Pathom chedi, Nakorn Pathom in the coronation pavilion of King Chulalongkorn at Wat Benchamabophit. This stupa of Sri Lankan style was erected by Rama IV in 1853 over a former stupa of the Dvaravati period, 6th century. It is about 120m (380ft) high and is the largest in Thailand. Built of brick and covered with glazed tiles, the architect of the project was Krom Khun Rajasinghavikrom, a member of the Chakri royal family. The stupa is surrounded by a circular cloister with *viharn* in the four cardinal directions.

ubosot in order to mark off the consecrated area. The roof was always of saddle type with tiles made of terracotta or glazed ceramic, and wood for provincial buildings. Gables of both *ubosot* and *viharn* sported carved figures of gods and floral motifs. In the reign of Rama III, some motifs and also the technique of making them were inspired by Chinese art and architecture, using fragments of Chinese ceramics. Ceilings were sometimes decorated with star motifs, gilded and inlaid with mirror and glass mosaic.

From the late 17th century onwards, records of the most important temples were kept. For example, it is noted that Wat Phra Sri Ratana Mahathat, Lopburi and Wat Boromphuttharam, Ayutthaya were roofed with yellow glazed tiles, probably imported from China. The bargeboards had the serpentine shape of the *naga* (mythical serpent) and the finial on the roof ridge at the gable top was in the form of the *naga* or garuda (mythical bird). These elements were made of wood, gilded and inlaid with glass mosaic. Some Sukhothai and Lan Na temples used glazed ceramic finials instead of wooden ones.

One of the best examples of a Thai temple compound symbolizing Buddhist cosmology is Wat Chaiwattanaram in the old capital of Ayutthaya. There is a main stupa in *prang* shape representing Mount Sumeru; it is surrounded by four small *prangs* representing the four continents at each corner on the same base. The square cloister surrounding it has eight more *prangs* which indicate the wall of the universe and the eight main directions.

Early royal architecture is more difficult to study because there are no records or remains. It has been suggested that early royal buildings were constructed of wood, thus explaining why there are none still extant. Only one valuable item that probably represents early royal architecture remains; it is the 9th-century stone *bai sema* found at Mueng Fadaed Songyang in Kalasin province which has a bas relief depicting the Buddha's visit to princess Bimba at her palace. Despite the lack of existing evidence, it is known that palace buildings were built as a cluster or group of houses similar to the layout of Thai domestic architecture. The buildings were on piles, and had curved boards fixed to the outer edge of the gable. They were placed in a compound with a wall and entrance was via a gate with a multi-storied roof.

Information, and even engravings, of Thai palaces from the Ayutthaya period are more plentiful. During this time foreigners were visiting Thailand for the first time, and they wrote about what they saw. Thai chronicles also mention royal buildings. It is known that brick became the material of choice for royal architecture in the mid 17th century when Ayutthaya had close contacts with western and Persian-Moghul architecture. The lime used to coat the buildings in this period is similar in technique and quality to that of buildings of that period in India.

A particular type of Thai royal architecture is the royal crematorium which was erected in wood. This non-permanent architectural structure in *prasat* shape was built occasionally when the king or members of the royal family died. Thai

Above: One of the four directional *viharn* around the *ubosot* at Wat Phra Chetuphon, Bangkok. The building with a row of square pillars on the right is the *ubosot*. It is enclosed by a wall with eight stone porticos. A pair of bronze mythical animals decorate each portico as symbolic door guardians. This temple was erected in the reign of Rama I and finished in 1801. It was restored and extended to its present scale in the reign of Rama III.

Left: Aerial view of Wat Yai Suwannaram, Thonburi, showing the *ubosot* surrounded by boundary stones (*bai sema*). Four small stupas situated at the corners of the wall probably represent the four continents of Buddhist cosmology or the four main directions.

records mention that some royal crematoria were 102.75m (330ft) tall. The oldest photographs of these royal structures were taken in the reign of Rama IV and Rama V, and they were 40m (130ft) tall. The royal crematorium also represents Buddhist cosmology.

Many materials — wood, brick, stucco and terracotta — were used in Thai architecture. Stone was the only material that wasn't widely utilized probably because the capitals of the Ayutthaya and Ratanakosin Kingdoms were situated in the alluvial plain where no suitable stone was available. At the same time, high quality woods such as teak were plentiful. Mirror, marble and coloured glazed tiles were new materials introduced to Thailand in the 17th century.

In the Ayutthaya period and thereafter, departments under royal patronage administered all the affairs related to the building of royal utensils, royal buildings and royal temples according to the king's wishes. They employed many specialized and talented craftsmen — sculptors, draughtsmen, founders, engravers, lacquer and plaster artists. This system ensured that the arts flourished in Thailand: work was centralized and skills and knowledge were handed down from one generation of artists to the next. Similarly, these artists took styles and techniques from the other cultures that they came into contact with, and incorporated these into their work. The result has been a more than 1000-year-old tradition of art and architecture with a real Thai identity, much of which remains to be admired today.

Left: A row of gilt bronze Buddha images in meditation, Ratanakosin style, early 19th century, in the cloister of Wat Suthat, Bangkok. A roofed walkway always surrounds an important edifice like a stupa or an *ubosot* in the sacred and public area of a temple.

Above: A cloister with gates surrounds various temple buildings in the sacred area of the Temple of the Emerald Buddha, Bangkok. The inner wall of the cloister is painted with scenes from the Thai version of the Ramayana, the Ramakien, in traditional Thai style.

Sukhothai

Sukhothai is the name of the kingdom of the northern area of present-day central Thailand which was founded in 1249. Sukhothai translates as 'Dawn of Happiness' probably referring to an era when the Thais first played an important role in this region. Three main rivers — the Ping, Yom and Nan — flow through this kingdom from the north to other territories in the south. Its major cities were situated in four directions from the capital, Sukhothai. These were Pitsanulok in the east, Si Satchanalai in the north, Kamphaeng Phet in the west and Nakornsawan in the south.

The Kingdom of Sukhothai played an independent role during nine successive reigns over two centuries until the late 15th century when it was occupied by the Ayutthaya Kingdom. The main factors that allowed it to prosper were skills in hydrology, the nature of the religious society, the Kingdom's function as an entrepot for trade for goods transported from the north to other countries in the south, peaceful relations with its neighbours and its growth as a centre for good quality glazed ceramic products.

Most Sukhothai cities have a moat and ramparts surrounding the settlement, but there was no specific rule for the plan of the town. Inside the city wall were ponds, the palace, houses and religious sanctuaries. The most important structure in the heart of each city seems to have been a Buddhist temple housing a relic of the Lord Buddha. These were Wat Mahathat in Sukhothai; Wat Phra Sri Ratana Mahathat, Pitsanulok; Wat Phrathat, Kampaeng Phet; and Wat Changlom, Si Satchanalai.

Stupas were built as repositories for the relic: The most popular shapes were the stupa in the shape of a lotus at the top, the Singhalese-influenced bell shape, and the Khmer *prang* shape.

There are no historical records on the palaces of Sukhothai rulers, but it has been suggested that the extant brick base opposite Wat Mahathat in Sukhothai was once the base of the wooden pavilion of a Sukhothai king. However, this theory was abandoned recently after an excavation by the Fine Arts Department suggested that it was from a temple building. Nevertheless, one of the stone slabs which decorated the ceiling of a rear passage at Wat Sri Chum north west of the city walls has an engraving of a multi-tiered roof similar in style to the royal *prasat* of a later period. It depicts a richly dressed person sitting in front, and is believed to be of a royal pavilion at Sukhothai that no longer exists.

Two main religions were practiced in Sukhothai: Hinduism and Buddhism, but Buddhism of the Hinayana sect was the more popular. Excavations at Sukhothai sanctuaries have found Hindu images at Wat Sri Sawai and Sarn Ta Pha Daeng. Also, from the early 13th century until the golden age of Hinayana Buddhism in the 14th century, Mahayana Buddhism which was practised in the Khmer Kingdom seems to have played an important role. Three *prang*–shaped buildings at Wat Phra Pai Luang are typical of Khmer Mahayana temples of the Jayavarman VII period, where the central *prang* housed a Buddha image and two side towers accommodated images of Bodhisattavas. At Hinayana Buddhist temples in Sukhothai the stupa was the most important building; it was always situated in the centre of the compound with the *viharn* in front. The *ubosot* was situated in a corner of the temple compound, and was sometimes built on a small island in a pond, as at Wat Traphang Ngoen and Wat Sra Sri. Some temples had a square *viharn* that housed the principal Buddha image. In these cases the *viharn* served as the main building in the temple instead of the stupa. At other sites a smaller rectangular *viharn* projected from the front of the building as at Wat Sri Chum. Most temple compounds were protected by a brick wall, seemingly promoting the separation between the secular world and the moral plane.

Religious architecture at Sukhothai evolved over time. In the early 13th century it was characterized by the Khmer styles of the *prasat* or *prang* type. Buildings during this period were made of laterite and surfaces were decorated with stucco motifs. Examples are the *prang* at Wat Sri Sawai and Wat Phra Phai Luang and the gate of a wall at Wat Phra Sri Ratana Mahathat, Sawankalok. By the early 14th century, Sukhothai had formed contact with several surrounding states such as Mon and Lan Na, and architectural influences from there began to appear. A good example is the subordinate stupa at Wat Chedi Chet Thew, Si Satchanalai. It is bell shaped on a raised square base and features a niche with a Buddha image in high relief. This type of stupa is of Pagan origin and reached Sukhothai via Lan Na.

One of the members of the Sukhothai royal family was a monk who went to Sri Lanka to study the Dharma with Buddhist scholars. After completing his studies, he returned

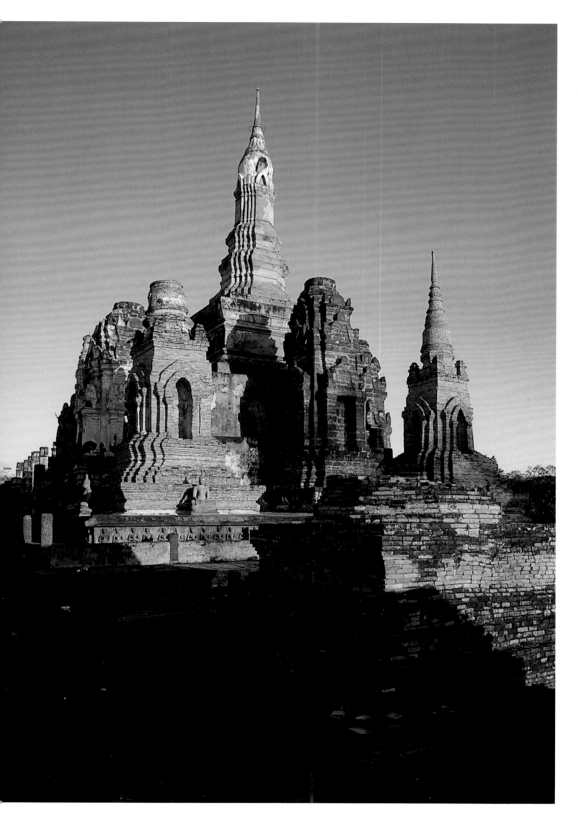

Above: Stucco bas reliefs decorate the top of the gate at Wat Phra Sri Ratana Mahathat, Sawankalok. The faces of the figures looking in the four directions are probably the faces of four guardian deities (*catummaharajika*). This style of image is influenced by Khmer architecture of the Jayavarman VII period. The stucco motif below the apex in foreground is the face of Rahu, the demon who is trying to swallow the moon.

Left: A significant form of Sukhothai architecture at Wat Mahathat is the lotus-shaped top of the stupa dating to the early 14th century. Its site is that of a principal building of the temple. There are eight smaller stupas in many shapes on the same base which probably represent the important directions of expansion of the Lord Buddha's doctrine.

Left: Wat Mahathat or The
Temple of the Great Relic,
Sukhothai. The key temple at
the heart of the settlement,
it is symbolic of Buddhist cosmology. It contained more
than 200 structures —stupa,
viharn, *ubosot* and so on —
and was surrounded by a low
brick wall.

to Sukhothai in 1334 and promoted Sri Lankan styles of art
and architecture in Sukhothai. Examples of this are the stucco
decoration displaying typically Sri Lankan motifs on a minor
prang built on the same base as the principal stupa at Wat
Mahathat; there is also a stupa in a bell shape and a stupa with
a ring of elephant sculptures encircling the base here too. From
the late 15th century, after Ayutthaya had totally occupied
Sukhothai, the Ayutthayan style of art and architecture began
to be seen. Examples inclue the *prang* at Wat Phra Sri Ratana
Mahathat, Sawankalok and the light slits in the walls at the
viharn of Wat Nang Phaya, Si Satchanalai.

Generally, the religious architecture of Sukhothai was not
large in scale. It had an air of understated calm and seemed
to be in harmony with its rural environment. It is as if the
builders were unwilling to display too strong an ambition.
This phenomenon accords with historical records that suggest
Sukhothai was primarily a religious society, not a materialist
one. Its main aim was to promote Hinayana Buddhism and
disseminate it in the surrounding Thai states.

Nonetheless, certain styles of architecture and decoration
became to be identified as 'Sukhothai style'. Brick walls or
moats surrounding religious buildings were the norm. The
stupa with a lotus-shaped top was pure Sukothai. And the
viharn with a high roof and narrow hall built to enshrine a
tall standing Buddha image, sometimes 9m (30ft) high, and
decorated with glazed ceramics of local manufacture, is
another example of an identifiable Sukhothai style.

Ayutthaya

Ayutthaya is the name given to the former capital and the Kingdom (1350–1767) whose boundaries correspond roughly to those of present-day Thailand. Ayutthaya was the capital for the longest period in Thai history. Founded in 1350 by King U-thong who probably moved down from Lopburi where there was a strong Khmer cultural influence, it is situated on an island surrounded by three main rivers. At its peak, there were three palaces and more than 100 temples inside the city, as well as countless temples outside the city walls. From the 16th century onwards foreign communities were established in separate enclaves along the river banks across from the city island. Such settlements were occupied by Portugese, Japanese, French, Dutch and those who practised the Islamic faith. When Ayutthaya was destroyed in 1767 by the Burmese, most of the buildings were set on fire; what little that was left fell into the ruins that now comprise the Ayutthaya Historical Park.

The most important palace at Ayutthaya was the Grand Palace in the north of the city. It consisted of four parts: The first was the area of the royal temple, Wat Phra Srisanphet, where three stupas stand in a row and have become the symbol of Ayutthaya. The second outermost area consisted of official buildings. The third middle area contained the three main *mahaprasat* (the tall sacred symbolic buildings for the God-King); each had a palatial spiral roof and they were used as royal residences and for royal ceremonies including the reception of foreign ambassadors. The final inner part of the palace was the private quarters of the king.

Left: The *ubosot* of Wat Salapoon, Ayutthaya with one of the boundary stones marking the limits of the sacred area. The architecture is typical of late 17th-century Ayutthaya architecture. Built of brick, the hall has an open pillared porch-verandah (*muk det*) projecting at the front. Roof edges are decorated with the serpentine shape of *naga* and the apex of the gable is topped with an elongated triangular finial (*cho fa*). The gable itself depicts a carved figure of a deity in the gesture of adoration.

Above: Stucco *singha* (lion) statues at the base of the bell-shaped stupa at Wat Thammikaraj, Ayutthaya. The crowned *singha* is very common in Khmer art as a door guardian protecting the sacred area. The figure symbolized a mythical animal that lived in the Himavana forest at the foot of Mount Sumeru.

Below: The gigantic base of the principal *prang* at Wat Chaiwatthanaram, west of the ancient city wall. The process of recessing the corner of a building was normal practice for Siamese architects as it gave the building an appearance of strength. With a height of 35m (110ft), the *prang* is the symbolic center of Buddhist cosmology and represents Mount Sumeru. Furthermore, it is ringed by quarter *prangs* and corner *prangs* connected by galleries, showing Khmer influence.

Right: A small, palatial style edifice in the style of a crematorium structure called a *meru* at Wat Chaiwatthanaram. Such *meru* were constructed at the four corners of a central *prang.* This temple was built in 1630 by King Prasatthong and dedicated to his mother.

Far right: Stucco sculptures of garuda in the gesture of raising their hands to carry something, and standing guardians decorate the corner of the *prang* above the main chamber at Wat Rajaburana, Ayutthaya. These sculptures are symbolic of attendants governed by moral principals.

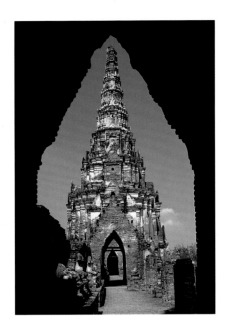

De la Loubère, the French envoy who visited Ayutthaya in 1686, mentioned in his description of Siam that the royal pavilions of the Ayutthaya palace were single-storey structures made of brick. He suggested that such brick buildings were introduced by westerners. He also mentions that their roofs were made of tin plate. Some Thai scholars suggest that the royal pavilions prior to King Narai the Great's reign (r 1656–1688) were wooden structures, but King Narai had them rebuilt in brick and also decorated the interior walls with gilt and glass mosaics. As these buildings were destroyed when the capital was attacked by the Burmese in 1767, it is not possible to ascertain this with any certainty. However, some of the royal pavilions made of wood, especially the private residences, were donated to monasteries when the owners died and therefore have been preserved. Two examples are the pavilion at Wat Yai Suwanaram constructed in the reign of King Pra Chao Sue (1703–1709) donated to a temple at Petchaburi, and the wooden pavilion with giltwork on the walls at Wat Sai, Thonburi, which was constructed in the same reign. Foreign visitors to Ayutthaya also mention that the garden areas in the palace contained foreign plants such as grapes, as well as fountains, a fish aquarium and a menagerie.

The main religion of Ayutthaya was Hinayana Buddhism. It was a Siamese tradition for the king or a wealthy person to illustrate their patronage of the religion by establishing a temple or dedicating a temple to themselves. This practice ensured that Ayutthaya had a huge number of temples, many of which

Left: Ruins of the *viharn* and stupa of *prang* shape at Wat Rajaburana, constructed in 1424. *Viharn* in Ayutthaya were considered much more important than *ubosot* so they were placed in front of the stupa. The frame of the door shows a *naga* element forming the door gable and a lion's leg motif decorates the base.

remain in varied states of repair today. The two most sacred temples in the city were Wat Phra Si Sanphet and Wat Mahathat: The former was in the Royal Palace compound and in one of its *viharn* is enshrined a 12-m (38-ft) standing Buddha image gilded with thin gold sheet. Wat Mahathat, on the other hand, was situated in the heart of the city and is famous for its towering stupa in the shape of a *prang*.

In planning temple layouts, architects were inspired by Buddhist cosmology. A stupa representing Mount Sumeru was erected in the middle of the compound. Within it was enshrined a Buddha relic. The *viharn* was always in front of the stupa and the *ubosot*, behind. This row of buildings always faced east and the area was surrounded by a cloister containing rows of Buddha images. The cloister represents the wall of the Buddhist universe. The monks' residential area (*sanghavasa*) was located in a separate part of the *wat* and contained many small wooden houses and a prayer hall.

The stupas of the Ayutthaya period have many shapes. In the early period, the *prang* shape showing the influence of Khmer architecture was very popular. Fine examples of this type can be seen at Wat Sorn and Wat Phutthaisawan. In these structures there are few corners and the body stands on a low base. Over time, this *prang* shape became taller and displayed many corners, as exemplified at Wat Rajaburana (1424). The bell-shaped stupa is another type which became popular when Sri Lankan Buddhism flourished in Ayutthaya from the early 15th century. These types of stupa were decorated with carved

Left: A window of a *hor trai* (a library building used as a repository for Buddhist manuscripts) which was originally at Ayutthaya but has been moved to Wat Sraket in Bangkok. Built in the late 17th to early 18th century, the window panels show the gilt gold process of European, probably French, origin. French artists introduced the idea of elegance into late 17th-century Ayutthaya art.

Right: Wooden model of a religious or sacrificial building in the late Ayutthaya style, *ca* late 17th century, with a horizontal line on the base and a roof that sags in the middle. Bangkok National Museum.

Above: The ceiling of the *ubosot,* Wat Na Phra Men, Ayutthaya, early 17th century, designed with carved wooden decoration elements, gilded and inlaid with glass mosaic.

symbolic motifs such as the *singha* (lion) and the garuda, mythical animals which live in the Himavana forest at the foot of Mount Sumeru.

The *viharn* and *ubosot* of Ayutthaya were built on a rectangular plan and always had few windows. The interiors were invariably dim, creating an atmosphere of peace and calm. Temple buildings with many windows were probably introduced by westerners in the 17th century. In order to show that such buildings were holy places, roofs were highly ornamental: they displayed gables with iconographical motifs in stucco or wood — such as Indra above three elephant heads signifying the Dusita Heaven. The tops of the capitals were always decorated with lotus petals in stucco in clustered or elongated shapes. Wooden brackets supporting the projecting eaves were ornately carved, normally in the shape of a *naga*. Door and window frames with pointed spires were made of stucco and gilded, while the panels were made of wood with varieties of decoration such as carving, mother-of-pearl inlay, and drawing by a gilding process. The bases of the *ubosot* and *viharn* in the late Ayutthaya period displayed horizontal lines sagging in the middle somewhat in the manner of a Chinese junk.

Inside the halls, pride of place was reserved for the principal Buddha image, normally sitting in the gesture of subduing Mara or in meditation. The interior walls were decorated with murals of the Jataka stories or lives of the Lord Buddha such as can be seen at Wat Chongnonsri in Bangkok. In fact, there

are many fine examples of Ayutthaya period buildings in provinces surrounding Ayutthaya — in Petchaburi, Lopburi, Nakorn Si Thammarat and Suphanburi.

From the founding of Ayutthaya in 1350 until its destruction in 1767, the Kingdom experienced 413 years as a mercantile marine port, so had plenty of exposure to other cultures through trade, war, religious encounters or diplomatic missions. Naturally Ayutthaya architecture reflects foreign influences. Stupas of the *prang* types are derived from Cambodia; some temple buildings have pointed arched windows and doors of Indo-Persian origin; European motifs decorate some *viharn* gables, as at Wat Tavej; bell-shaped stupas taken from Sri Lankan architecture were very popular in Ayutthaya in the early 15th century; and the base of the stupa at Wat Phu Kaothong is similar in style to that of a Mon-Burmese stupa. By taking these architectural features from other cultures and mixing them with their own unique Thai styles, the Siamese of Ayutthaya built a splendid city with what has become known as a uniquely Ayutthaya identity.

Above: The principal Buddha image in the *viharn* at Wat Sao Tongtong, Lopburi. The plan of the building is not rectangular, the normal Siamese *viharn* shape, but instead is square at the rear projecting into a rectangular chamber. The wall has many pointed arched niches inspired by Indo-Persian art, an architectural style commonly employed on doors and windows in King Narai the Great's reign in the late 17th century. Some scholars have suggested that this building may have been a Muslim mosque which was converted to a Buddhist *viharn* in a later period.

Opposite: Seated Buddha image in the gesture of subduing Mara, at Wat Phananchoeng, Ayutthaya. The Ayutthaya Chronicle mentions that this temple was built 26 years before Ayutthaya was founded by King U-Thong in 1350. The Buddha image, 13m (55ft) high, is made of stucco and gilded with gold leaf. Buddhists still make merit by offering robes to this Buddha image.

Right: The principal gate of the palace connecting the inner court with the central court. There are eight gates in the same style. The Indo-Persian pointed arch is the door entrance. The door is quite high because the main vehicle of the period was the elephant. The many niches in the wall of the gate were for oil lamps. The pathway was finished in brick. The laying of a pathway instead of a staircase to reach a higher level was more convenient for those carrying a palanquin.

Narai Palace, Lopburi

By the middle of the 17th century, the Kingdom of Siam or Ayutthaya had been in existence for three centuries. There began a period of economic and political stability and a flowering of culture and the arts which can truly be called a golden era. Siam became one of the most famous kingdoms in the East. Envoys from several places including Aceh, Batavia, Persia, Portugal, Holland, the Moghul Empire and France established diplomatic and commercial ties with the kingdom, while many foreigners such as Portuguese, Malay, Japanese, Chinese and Dutch settled near the capital, Ayutthaya. This brought the Siamese more knowledge about world affairs and also offered them the opportunity to exchange experiences with different nationalities.

One of the Siamese kings in the 17th century who supported the policy of opening Siam to the world was King Narai the Great (r 1656–1688). He sent envoys to the courts of King Louis IV of France, Sultan Sulaiman of Persia and the Kang-Hsi Emperor of China, and in return many countries sent similar embassies to Siam. Thus Narai was able to invite technocrats, engineers, physicians, architects and scientists from abroad to work on some of his pet projects.

One such project was the renovation and expansion of the city of Lopburi. King Narai enjoyed the attractive climate and elephant hunting opportunities in Lopburi, and spent the greater part of each year there. In 1666, work began on the Palace at Lopburi. Encompassing an area of 42 rai (7 hectares) and facing east, it was surrounded by a tall brick crenellated

Opposite: Chanthara Phisan Hall is the only building in this palace which has no windows or doors in the shape of pointed arches. One scholar suggested that this typically Thai architecture shows it was the first building erected in the palace compound. The small projecting annex to the main building is a typical form of architecture from the King Narai period. It is a small throne chamber used for receiving officials or envoys.

Left: Chantara Phisan of the King Narai period and the rear part of Phiman Mongkut of the King Mongkut (Rama IV) period (on right). The gable of King Mongkut's pavilion is decorated with a stucco crown motif, the regalia of King Mongkut.

Above: The front part of Phiman Mongkut Hall, built in 1856 during the reign of King Mongkut. It comprises several halls connected to each other. The roof of the building shows Chinese influences, a style that became popular for royal and religious buildings from the Third reign onwards. A low wall with a row of niches for oil lamps is seen in the front.

wall. The rear of the palace lined the Lopburi river, the main route to Ayutthaya. Even though there are a variety of architectural styles, such as arched windows showing Persian and Moghul influences and a hydraulic water pipe system designed by Italian engineers, the palace compound itself was laid out according to traditional Siamese palace plans and divided into three areas.

The outer part was the area for government duty and general works. There was a court of justice, storerooms for export goods, a reception hall for envoys, elephant stables and a Buddhist shrine for the Palace. Descriptions by French and Persian visitors talk of square gardens with fountains decorating the area. The central courtyard, which was described by a French visitor as being more beautiful than the outer part of the palace, consisted of two main buildings: the first which was called Dusitsawan Thanyamahaprasat was a throne hall with a pointed roof; it was used to welcome the French ambassadors, the Chevalier de Chaumont in 1682 and de la Loubère in 1687, and the ambassador from Persia, Ibrahim Beg in 1686. The second building was a meeting hall for high officials named Chanthara Phisan.

The third area of the palace was the inner court comprising King Narai the Great's private quarters. It was closed to the general public, but a French visitor mentioned that there were fountains of various shapes here and some of the plants were tended by the king himself. Today only one building named Sutthasawan still remains. It is where the king died on 11 July

Above: The area of the inner court of King Mongkut in the former Palace of King Narai the Great. The central building, the Royal Meeting Hall, is in the style of Thai architecture of the 17th century. On either side are buildings for the ladies of the court of King Mongkut. The doors and windows are similar to those of an old Thai-style house but the ground floor displays European influences.

Left: Phiman Mongkut building, with a high roof over the central part which was a throne hall. The gable here is decorated with a stucco motif of a throne under the royal umbrella.

Left: An engraving of the Throne Hall recorded by the French in de la Loubère's book *Du Royaume de Siam*. It is mentioned that the wall of the throne hall of King Narai the Great was decorated with mirrors which were brought from France by his envoy. The style of the room is similar to that of the existing Dusit Sawan Thanyamahaprasat and was probably inspired by La Salle de Grace in the Palace at Versailles.

Right: The Dusitsawan Thanyamahaprasat building is divided into two parts: The front section is the hall for granting audiences with foreign envoys; it displays high pointed arches on the windows and doors in the Indo–Persian style. At the rear are two staircases leading to a raised platform for the throne of King Narai. Even though King Narai the Great died more than 300 years ago, local people believe that his sacred spirit still occupies this throne chamber.

1688. A few months before he died, however, he was overthrown by some of his ministers in a *coup d'état*. The new king, Phra Phetraja, brought the court back to the capital, Ayutthaya, and Lopburi declined in importance thereafter. Many of its buildings including the palace were abandoned or neglected, and fell into ruins.

In the mid 19th century King Mongkut (Rama IV), the fourth sovereign of the Chakri Dynasty who reigned from 1851 to 1868, was faced with the threat of colonization by the western powers. Because it was so close to the sea, the capital Bangkok was susceptible to attack by gun-boat, so King Mongkut decided to choose an alternative site for a second capital in case of an emergency. Lopburi was the site he selected.

In 1856 he began renovations on the palace of King Narai the Great. Some old buildings dating from King Narai's reign which were in ruins — such as Chantara Phisan — were restored as complete buildings. Other new buildings were added in the central courtyard, such as Phiman Mongkut Pavilion and buildings for the king's consorts. The style of architecture at this time was a mixture of Chinese, Western and Thai — and the end result reflects this eclectic mix. After King Mongkut's reign the palace at Lopburi was handed over to the provincial government for offices and later became a museum.

Ratanakosin Temple Architecture

After the collapse of Ayutthaya following the Burmese invasion in 1767, King Taksin (r 1767–1782) established a new capital at Thonburi on the west bank of the Chao Phraya river. It was around 70 km (45 miles) south of the former capital and more accessible from the Gulf of Siam than Ayutthaya had been. However, in 1782, when King Rama I succeeded to the throne, he decided to move his palace to the opposite bank of the river and named this new centre Krung Ratanakosin Inayothaya (present-day Bangkok). Ratanakosin means 'a place for precious gems', because the famous Emerald Buddha was to be housed here. This name is now commonly used for referring to the present period of Thai history, which began in 1782.

Ordinary Thai people suffered greatly during the centuries of war, but their strong belief in Buddhism never diminished. To start their new settlement, they had to think about the ideals of their society, above all the ideas of religion and kingship, and the relationship between the two. Construction began in earnest in 1783. The most sacred temple of the kingdom is the Temple of the Emerald Buddha, first established in the palace compound. The second most sacred is the great temple in the heart of the city known as Wat Suthat. During the reigns of Rama I to Rama V, each king built a temple to commemorate his reign, beginning with Wat Phra Chetuphon built by Rama I.

Because the scale of the new capital was so immense, a Royal Crafts Department was created to oversee construction. Sited in the palace, it was headed by a high ranking person. (Rama II while he was a prince was appointed by King Rama I

Above: On the perimeter of Ratanakosin Island stand many old temples of the Early Ratanakosin period. Wat Sakret, characterized by a bell-shaped stupa on the top of a high base, is one. Another is the temple consisting of three buildings — two *viharn* and an *ubosot* in the middle; it dates from King Rama III's reign and was dedicated to this monarch's favourite niece. The area is the main entrance to the city, so more buildings in the style of a hall without a wall were constructed recently as reception halls for state visits and receptions.

Right: The *ubosot* and curved balcony at Wat Rajabopit, a symbolic temple for King Rama V. The special material used for this temple is a glazed tile of five colours decorating the walls of the buildings.

Right: Splendid motifs on a wooden bas relief decorate the gables of a building at Wat Suthat. Vishnu above a garuda and Indra above Airavanta are symbolic motifs that represent a Hindu divinity and the Chakaravatin (Universal Emperor).

to act as head.) With a new ruler, a new capital and a new dynasty (Rama I was the first monarch of the Chakri Dynasty), the building of Krung Ratanakosin Inayothaya heralded the dawn of a new era. Many temples from this early Ratanakosin period were built on a large scale and were intended to showcase the ideals of this new spiritual and social atmosphere.

The architectural style of Ratanakosin temples falls into three main categories. In the first phase, buildings followed the formulae of the past — the Ayutthaya style. This is evident in many instances — in the decorated gable motifs and curved base of the *ubosot* at the Temple of the Emerald Buddha or in the wooden bas reliefs present on many gables of buildings at Wat Phra Chetuphon or Wat Suthat. A motif such as Vishnu above the garuda is a symbol of a moral king and reflects the philosophy of Siamese society. Another such motif is a figure in the gesture of adoration symbolizing a deity in the heavens. The first large stupa at Wat Phra Chetuphon built in the reign of King Rama I to contain the relics of the sacred standing Buddha brought from Ayutthaya, copied the stupa of King Prasat Thong's reign at Ayutthaya.

This continuity of traditional Ayutthaya architectural style lasted until the end of King Rama II's reign, some 30 years later. In the early 19th century, the kingdom of Siam stabilized. There were fewer wars, more stable internal politics and Rama III had close commercial contacts with South China. These phenomena brought chinoiserie to Siam. Temple architecture began to sport the use of ceramic fragments, such as Chinese

Top: The Ratanakosin Era offers a plethora of different styles of gable motifs in temple buildings: These are from two early Ratanakosin buildings and are (on left) Buddha in meditation under the hood of a *naga*, (on right) a climbing plant motif set around adoring divinities. Both gables courtesy of Neold, Bangkok.

Above: Wooden bas relief covered in gold leaf depicts a scene from the Ramakien, the Thai version of the Ramayana. A *yaksha* (ogre converted to the service of Buddhism) is fighting a troop of monkeys on a gable at Wat Phra Chetuphon.

Far left: Pillars of a temple building at Wat Suthat decorated with glazed tiles. The top of the pillars are in the shape of lotus petals. Wooden brackets supporting the projecting eaves are ornately carved with *naga*.

Left: An ornate window of the *ubosot* at Wat Rajabophit with *mondop*-shaped niches. The window panels display royal Thai decorative motifs.

Below: It is very common to decorate religious architecture with carved wood and stucco motifs, gilt and inlaid with glass mosaic, as on the *viharn* at Wat Rajabophit, early 19th century.

Opposite: Prasat Phra Thepbidon at the Temple of the Emerald Buddha was erected in the reign of King Rama IV. The walls of the building are decorated with coloured glass. The window frame is in the shape of the royal Siamese crown-spire, called *mongkut* in Thai, which is also the name of the King who erected the building.

blue and white, inlaid in the stucco. More commonly, the roofs took on Chinese characteristics, the famous *prang* of Wat Arun being but one example. *Naga* or *cho fa* gable decorations were replaced by Chinese-inspired motifs, such as stucco dragons or griffins. Many sculptures, such as door guardians, and even architectural structures like door frames, were imported from China. Fine examples of this chinoiserie architecture can be seen at Wat Rajaoros, Wat Theptidaram and Wat Kallayanmit. However, it is important to note that this style was not pure Chinese, but a mixture of Thai and Chinese elements.

After this era, Thai religious architecture divided into two styles. During the reign of King Rama IV (1851–1868), there was a return to more traditional Thai forms, as a reflection of his personal taste. The 120-m (380-ft) Great Stupa in Nakorn Pathom and the Prasat Pra Thepbidon or Royal Pantheon (1855) in the Temple of the Emerald Buddha are two good examples of this. But in the reign of Rama V (1868–1910), in a more westernized cultural situation than in former times, some monasteries were erected in a pure western style. The *ubosot* at Wat Nivet Thammapravat is in the Gothic style, and the interiors of Wat Rajabophit and the stained glass window gable at Wat Benchamabopit are clearly Western-influenced.

The religious architecture of the Ratanakosin period from 1782 to the present day combines the traditional style from Ayutthaya, with influences from China and the west. These later phenomena occurred because of the personal aesthetic tastes of the supreme powers of the kingdom, the kings.

Right: An interior view of the *ubosot* of Wat Phra Kaew (the Temple of the Emerald Buddha) on Chakri Memorial Day, awaiting the arrival of the king. The Emerald Buddha is considered to be the holiest Buddha image in the Ratanakosin Kingdom. It is 26cm (10in) high and is in the 15th-century Lan Na style. It is set on a high base in the shape of a *prasat* (a building designed to illustrate the importance of a king). The *prasat* is covered with gold leaf. In front of this *prasat*- stands a pair of crowned Buddha images in the gesture of dispelling fear. These two images were made by King Rama III and were dedicated to King Rama I and Rama II. The walls inside the *ubosot* are decorated with a mural depicting the story of the lives of the Lord Buddha.

Below: Inside one of the *viharn* at Wat Borvornivet are housed standing Buddha images. This small *viharn* was built in the reign of Rama IV. The interior wall is painted with scenes from the 'Romance of the Three Kingdoms' which was very popular in the early Ratanakosin Period.

The Royal Palace, Bangkok

Many consider that the royal palace in Bangkok is the apogee of Thai architecture. At the same time it is a fine example of an architectural entity that reflects Thai ideas about Buddhism and also Hindu cosmology.

In 1782, after Rama I seized the throne from King Taksin, the new monarch decided to move the royal palace from Thonburi to a site on the opposite bank of the river, where the present palace still stands. The reasons for this were twofold: Firstly, because of the surrounding loop of the river the new site was larger; and secondly, a new king needed a new residence. It was deemed inauspicious for Rama I to remain in the palace that the former king had occupied.

Thai culture is strongly identified with ancestral practices. For the founding of a new grand palace, many old formulae passed down from palace architecture of Ayutthayan times had to be followed. The size of the new palace had to be nearly the same as the old one; the river had to flow on the right side of the palace wall; and the royal temple had to stand inside the palace compound. Most importantly, the palace had to be an extremely elaborate building with a tall spiral roof, the top of which could clearly be seen from the main arterial waterway, the Chao Phraya river. Moreover, the compound had to be surrounded by a high brick wall decorated with *bai sema* and fronted by a wide open space. These two factors indicated that the area was a 'separated area', and as such it was a holy place.

Construction of the palace began in 1787 with the erection of two main buildings: the Phra Thinang Indra Phisek, the *prasat*

Above: A small pavilion, Phra Thinang Chaichumpol, constructed in the reign of King Rama IV on the top of the palace wall on the eastern side. It is used for observing parades and soldiers training. The building's walls can be opened wide on every side in order to make it an open hall.

Right: Sala Prueng Krueng, a minor annex connected to the Phra Thinang Dusit Mahaprasat by bridge, was built in 1922 in the reign of Rama VI. The stucco motif on the door frames and windows is in the shape of a floating basket (up and down) which has been popular since the reign of King Narai in the 17th century.

Right: Phra Thinang Dusit Mahaprasat was erected in the reign of Rama I with a seven-tiered spire above four levels of saddle roofs symbolizing the god's *vimarn* transfer to the earth as God-King. This is one of the best examples of traditional Thai symbolic architecture extant in the country. The front part of the building projects an open small porch in which the Busabokmala throne stands. The two L-shaped buildings in front of the Phra Thinang are where officers and courtiers withdraw to and remain during the appearance of the king at the porch. This area is surrounded by a low wall demarking it as a sacred area. The entrance to the pavilion is through the gate with a tiered spire roof. A pair of stone lions flanking either side of the entrance are the protective door guardians.

building with a multi-storied roof, and a group of buildings called Muu Phra Mahamontien. The former was an architectural symbol of the presence of the God-King and was used for audiences and as a ceremonial hall; the latter were used as a hall of residence and halls of audience. More than 200 years have passed since the inception of the palace; over time many buildings have been added and some of the older existing structures have undergone restoration. Today's palace reflects a diversity of architectural features from different cultures that influenced Thai society at various times as well as the personal stylistic tastes of succeeding monarchs.

The early buildings followed the Ayutthaya formula, but a few decades later during the reign of Rama III, as a result of increased trade between Siam and South China, the influence of Chinese architecture becomes apparent. In the mid 19th century, western architectural tastes affected the Siamese elite who felt they had to adapt their styles in order to survive in the modern world. Many buildings in the palace which were erected in this period reflect the western neo-classic or Victorian styles.

The palace faces north while the royal temple faces east (the north and the east are auspicious directions in Thai religious belief). The palace encompasses an area of 182 rai (30 hectares) and is divided into four areas: the royal temple and the outermost, middle and innermost areas. The most interesting of these is the middle area consisting of a number of royal pavilions, the most outstanding of which is the Dusit Mahaprasat: It has a ground-floor plan of cruciform shape

with a multi-storied roof placed at the intersection of the saddle roofs. This building replaced the original Indraphisek which was burned down in 1789. The pavilion was roofed with tin plate and replaced by coloured glazed tiles in the reign of Rama III. The gable depicts a carved figure of Vishnu above Garuda, gilded and ornamented with glass mosaic inlay.

Muu Phra Mahamontien which means 'royal residence' comprises many halls of audience, a bed chamber and palace shrines which are inter-connected. The building has many levels of saddle roofs and two overlapping eaves on each side, while the roof tiles are color glazed. The gables depict carved figures of Indra mounted on Airavanta — representing the building in the Dusita heaven. Some of the interior walls were painted in the reign of Rama III. The building is surrounded by a low wall with doors in the *prasat* shape. All these details indicate that the Muu Phra Mahamontien, except for the God-King area, represents the non-secular world.

The Phra Thinang Chakri Mahaprasat is another royal building in the middle area which is attractive because its style combines western neo-classicism with the classic Thai roof with royal spire. This building was started in 1875 under the supervision of two English architects from Singapore, John Clunish and Henry Clunish Rose, and completed in 1882. King Rama V who favoured western architecture used this building as his residence and as an audience hall.

The inner court is the area at the rear of the middle court where the apartments of the royal consorts stand. The build-

Above: Hor Phra Prit or Hor Sastrakom in the foreground and also other royal buildings in the Grand Palace showing different styles of roof, wall and structure. The Hor Phra Prit has a gable decorated with a carved wood deity holding a sword. The Buddha image used in ritual chants is housed inside the building.

Left: The entrance to the Muu Phra Mahamontien in the shape of a crowned spire roof was erected in the reign of Rama IV. It is decorated with colourful glazed ceramic fragments. The gate is flanked in front by two stone lion door guardians. Behind the gate are the saddle roofs and overlapping eaves of the Muu Phra Mahamontien which is covered with coloured glazed tiles.

Below: Originally built as an open pavilion, Phra Thinang Dusidaphirom was constructed in the reign of Rama I inside a walled area of the Muu Phra Mahamontien. It is used by the reigning monarch as a robing chamber before making a journey by palanquin or for mounting an elephant. The building has been renovated several times and the glass window was probably installed in the Rama V period. The outstanding feature of this building is the interior and exterior wall painting.

ings here include small brick group houses displaying Chinese architectural features, especially at the door entrances which were popular for the inner court buildings in the reigns of Rama III–IV. The architecture also shows European neo-classic or baroque styles in the buildings used by important consorts. Such European influences were popular in the fifth reign.

In the early 20th century towards the end of Rama V's reign, it was decreed that Bangkok's glamorous Grand Palace was too crowded. The King decided to erect a new palace in the European style in a suburb of Bangkok. Both the royal palace and park were called the Dusit palace. Since then, succeeding monarchs have continued the practice of not confining themselves to one permanent residential palace. Even with this changed situation, the Grand Palace still plays an important role as the symbolic sacred seat of the reigning Thai monarch and it is the place where royal ceremonies are performed: the coronation, royal funeral rites, royal audiences, provision of accommodation for state visits and state banquets. As such, it is still alive and imbued with the spirit of Thai tradition.

Opposite: A long gallery of the front audience hall of Phra Thinang Chakri Mahaprasat.

Above: The east private room, Phra Thinang Chakri Mahaprasat, used as a reception room for royal guests. On one wall hangs a large portrait of Rama V, the Queen and the five princes, which was painted in 1897 by Edoardo Gelli from a photograph in Florence, Italy during the King's first visit to Europe.

Left: The royal palanquin of carved ivory, placed in the reception hall of Phra Thinang Chakri Mahaprasat belongs to the Rama V period. The pillow placed on it depicts the garuda motif which is believed to be the vehicle of the Lord Vishnu, the incarnation of the God-King.

Right: The interior of the southern chamber of the Phra Thinang Dusit Mahaprasat which housed the two thrones — the window shaped throne with the *prasat* designed frame of the Rama IV period at the rear and the throne inlaid with mother-of-pearl of the Rama I period placed in the front. A nine-tiered white umbrella surmounts the throne and symbolizes kingly power extending to the nine directions, the eight cardinal directions and the upwards direction, but some have suggested that it represents the Hinayana Buddhist monarch such as is found in Thailand, Burma, Laos and Cambodia. The gold and silver trees surrounding the throne were presents from vassal states, but some argue that they represent the golden and silver trees at the foot of Mount Sumeru.

Opposite: The front throne hall of the Phra Thinang Amarin Winitchai where the two thrones of King Rama I were placed. At the rear is the boat shaped throne, Busabok Maha Chakrapat Piman. In front is a square throne surmounted with a nine-tiered white umbrella. Both are of gilded carved wood with an inlaid gold and glass mosaic. Many small sculptures such as a lion garuda and *deva* decorate the base of the throne representing it as Mount Sumeru. Sometimes this audience hall is used for ceremonies such as merit-making dedications to past kings by the placing of royal urns on the throne, as can be seen in this picture.

Left: The central throne hall of the Phra Thinang Chakri Mahaprasat is unique for its display of eastern- and western-inspired opulence, both styles working together. The throne is of gold niello and was presented to King Rama V by a ruler of Nakorn Si Thammarat, famous for its gold niello production. Behind the throne is a painting of a *chakra* and a *trisula*, the holy weapons of the Hindu gods and symbolic of the Ratanakosin Chakri Dynasty. On either side of the throne are two deities holding the king's sword and the royal signet casket. Two mythical animals, *rajasi* and *kojjasi*, flank either side and represent the absolute power of the monarchy that stands above civil (*rajasi*) and military (*kojjasi*) administration.

Lan Na Temple Architecture

Lan Na or 'Land of a Million Ricefields' was the name of one of the Thai city-states in the present-day north of Thailand which now comprises eight provinces. This state came into being when King Mengrai from Chiang Rai moved down to occupy the area of the Ping river where an older Mon state called Haripunchai (present-day Lamphun) was situated. After consolidating vast tracts of territory that even extended into parts of Burma and Laos, he proclaimed himself King of Lan Na and in 1296 commenced work on building his capital at Chiang Mai. As the Kingdom of Lan Na was a buffer state between the two most powerful kingdoms in the region — Burma and Siam — it had to have a cultural and political policy that was harmonious with both kingdoms. However, in the late 18th century, Lan Na formed an alliance with Siam and became its tributary.

A search for a national identity and also cultural interaction with her neighbours are reflected in Lan Na's 700 years of history. In the early days, the main religion of the Lan Na people was Hinayana Buddhism, but between the late 14th and early 15th centuries, Sri Lankan Buddhism exerted a strong influence in the region. This was through Buddhist missionaries from Sukhothai (who had originally come from Sri Lanka) and pilgrims from Chiang Mai visiting and studying in what was then Ceylon. Unsurprisingly, features of Sri Lankan architectural style appear in Lan Na architecture.

Lan Na temples differed from their southern counterparts in many ways. Temple sites were specific, such as in the centre

Above: The stupa that houses the principal Buddha image in the *viharn* Luang at Wat Phra That Lampang Luang, Lampang constructed in 1496. The stupa is decorated with a stucco motif and gilded with gold leaf.

Right: Inside the mid 16th-century *viharn* Nam Tam at Wat Phra That Lampang Luang are an array of Buddha images of different gestures on a large base. The wall behind the images is decorated with gilt motifs of Bodhi trees, floral designs, the moon, the sun and various deities on black lacquer.

Above: The *viharn* Nam Tam at Wat Phra That Lampang Luang, Lampang is one of the finest examples of a Lan Na *viharn*. Mural paintings of local literature decorate the upper surface of the side walls of the building. The *cho fa*, the decorative roof element sitting on top of the gable, is in typical Lan Na style and points straight up into the sky.

Left: Wat Phra Singh in Chiang Mai is one of the most revered temples in Lan Na because it houses an important Buddha image named Phra Singh. First erected by King Payu in 1340, the temple compound has many stupa and *viharn*.

Below: Wat Pongsanuk Tai in Lampang is situated on a slight hill. The boundary of the temple is reached by walking up a staircase with a *naga* balustrade representing a pathway connecting earth and heaven. The gate, decorated with a stucco motifs, is the second important stage reached before entering the sacred area.

of a village or city or on the highest part of a settlement. Normally there was a wall surrounding the temple area with a splendid brick gate leading to the *viharn*. Behind the *viharn* was the stupa. Lan Na people believed that the *ubosot* building should be used only for monks' ceremonies, so it was always small and sometimes one *ubosot* served several temples. The position of the *ubosot* and also the *hor pra traipidok* or temple library to house sacred books might be beside the *viharn*.

A study of Lan Na temple architecture needs to take into account the development of the stupa and the *viharn*. The earliest type of Lan Na stupa in the early 13th century was in the shape of a rectangular structure decorated with ornate niches and standing on a high base. On the top was a bell-shaped structure with a pointed spire with other smaller bell-shaped structures at the corners. Good examples of this style of stupa can be seen at Wat Chiangyan, Lamphun and Wat Pasak, Chiang Saen. The second style of Lan Na stupa, popular in this area in the late 14th century, is also bell shaped but in the Sri Lankan style. The stupas at Wat Suandok and Wat U-Mong, Chiang Mai, are examples of this style. This type of stupa later developed a high base with several layers; a good example is the stupa at Wat Prathat Haripunchai in Lamphun, which was renovated in 1447. Many important stupas in other Lan Na cities, such as the one at Prathat Cheh-heang, Nan Province, were inspired by this type.

In the early 16th century, the style of stupa in Lan Na was unique for its high rectangular base, as can be observed on the

Below: Gilt motif of a vase with vines (*purana kalasa*) symbolic of prosperity on a black lacquer surface on the front wall of the *viharn* Phra Phut, Wat Phra That Lampang Luang. This *viharn* was erected in the late 15th century.

Right: Lan Na door panels of the *viharn* at Wat Lai Hin, Lampang. A carved wooden plaque with a floral design hides the top part.

Far right: A wooden bracket supporting the projecting eaves of the same *viharn*. It is carved with a dragon design and chrysanthemum leaves, an auspicious symbol of Chinese origin.

Opposite: Inner sanctuary of the same *viharn* where the principal Buddha image stands in the centre. The Buddha is in the gesture of subduing Mara. Wooden and cloth materials form a hanging banner signifying veneration of the Lord Buddha.

stupas at Wat Molilok and Wat Prathat Doi Suthep, Chiang Mai. Some stupas were influenced by Sukhothai architecture and decorated with elephant images on the first level of the base, such as at the stupa at Wat Chiengmun, Chiang Mai. A significant feature of the Lan Na stupa is its surface of thin metal sheet covered with gold leaf.

The *viharn* in Lan Na was always erected in front of the most important spot in the temple, the stupa, and faced east. The oldest extant Lan Na *viharn* is one without an external wall, at Wat Phra That Lampang Luang in Lampang. However, later, *viharn* were always constructed with walls. Originally, roof tiles were either of terracotta or flat pieces of teak. Roofs were highly decorative, and often displayed a *prasat* in the middle of the main roof ridge as a symbol of Mount Sumeru. A carved wooden panel decorated with lacquer gilding and glass mosaics in the form of two arches meeting at a center was fixed under the gable. Triangular slab brackets of different designs supported the projecting eaves.

In order to expose the timber structure of the roof, the *viharn* usually had no ceiling except in the place directly above the Buddha image. As a sign of respect, the ceiling here was always decorated in geometric patterns of small wooden squares with intricate floral and vegetal motifs. Sometimes, murals decorate the interior walls. Another technique to decorate a wall, pillar and roof structure of a *viharn* was the use of floral, mythical animals and deity designs in gold leaf on black lacquer.

Opposite: The principal Buddha image in the *viharn* at Wat Po Pichit, Chiang Mai. The ceiling above the Buddha image is decorated with a small square pattern and floral and geometric gilt motifs.

Right: Wooden roof structure decorated with gilt motifs at the *viharn* at Wat Pong Yang Kok, Lampang. The structure shows how the weight of the roof is balanced across the building.

Right below: The ceiling above the Buddha image area inside the *viharn* of Wat Pumin, Nan. It is patterned with small square designs with wood cuts in a star shape.

Overleaf: Wat Chiang Mun, Chiang Mai, marking the site of King Mengrai's earliest settlement. This temple is a good example of Lan Na temple buildings because it comprises a *viharn*, *ubosot*, scripture library and stupa.

The ordinary Lan Na *viharn* was built to house a Buddha image in front of the rear wall of the building, but there are two more special types of *viharn* in Lan Na which differ from those in other regions in Thailand. These are the *viharn* built to house a small stupa inside and those that have an annex with a *mondop*, a square building with a palatial spired roof. In both cases, the small stupa and *mondop* have a room to house the Buddha image. Examples of these can be observed at Wat Chomthong, Wat Padaeng Luang, Wat Prasat and Wat Phra Singh, all in Chiang Mai.

In summary, Lan Na temple architecture evolved over centuries largely in isolation from other Kingdoms in Thailand. As such, it is highly individualistic. However, many of its forms display influences from Ayutthaya, Sukhothai and Burma, and also Sri Lanka. Many highly distinctive buildings are extant.

Classic Thai Design & Craftsmanship

Thais have an innate sense of beauty which extends even to the smallest of objects and allows them to create not only designs that are particularly Thai but also modify those of others so that they attain a Thai character. Concurrent with this is a mastery of craftsmanship honed over millennia.

First and foremost, artists and artisans create objects of beauty to the best of their ability to venerate and dedicate to the Buddha and the monarchy. They vie to produce the most imaginative of decorations and ceremonies to honour these two most important influences on their lives. The production of art objects of special design and craftsmanship for wealthy patrons obviously is of importance too. Creation of beauty for loved ones, such as the making of special garments by mothers for sons ordaining as monks, has an important role. Then, of course, there are the utilitarian goods that are a necessity. Among the objects created are temple murals, banners and furnishings, manuscripts and scripture cabinets and chests, the latter two often bearing gilded designs on lacquer, silver, mother-of-pearl and niello ceremonial containers, jewelry, coins, textiles, ceramics and most important, Buddha images.

It is now estimated that the casting of bronze in Thailand began in 1500–1000 BCE in Ban Chiang and other sites in north-eastern Thailand with adzes and spearheads being cast in open and bivalve moulds. However, excavations at Ban Na Di, another prehistoric site near Ban Chiang, prove two types of casting were used there, one with bivalve moulds and the other the 'lost wax'. The latter found its highest expression in the great seated and walking Sukhothai Buddha images. Two methods may be employed in the lost wax process, depending on whether a hollow or solid statue is to be cast. Large images are usually hollow cast because of technical and economical reasons.

In hollow casting a core of clay is first roughly formed. This is then covered with a mixture of clay and shellac of the required thickness desired for the finished image (usually 1–25mm; less than an inch). Then the mixture is worked to form the features and details desired in the finished image. This is covered with three layers, all dried each after the other, to form a mould. The first is a mixture of cow dung, fine clay and other ingredients. The second and third layers are composed of increasingly coarse clay and sand. Solid cast images have no clay core. Instead the model is made entirely of wax and then etched to form the proper details and covered with three of the same types of coats as for the hollow castings. In both the hollow and solid statue casting the clay mould is placed on a furnace for the wax to melt. When completed, the mould is turned upside down for the wax to flow out, then uprighted and returned to the furnace. Then the mould is filled from crucibles of molten metal. When the mould has cooled it is broken and the image freed. Finally, the finishing work includes the complete removal of the clay mould, the chiselling away of the pipes and nails, the correction of casting errors and polishing of the image. The final stage is the gilding, where thin leaves of gold are applied to a surface ground with a layer of lacquer.

Buddha images are ritually imbued with *teja* or fiery energy, which is activated in a ceremony devised for the image's consecration. The spirit of the Buddha is invited to reside in his likeness. Only then does the image transcend the material and is no longer just a physical object but is considered a living being with an inner spirit.

Pottery in Thailand may have begun as early as 5500 BCE as is suggested by potsherds in the top layer of human occupation, Spirit Cave, northwestern Thailand. In around 2100 BCE

wares with impressive Neolithic incised designs made their appearance in Ban Chiang and other sites throughout much of Thailand. Figurines of animals have been found in Bronze Age burials including one of an infant. The above and later pottery with painted designs in red *circa* 300 BCE to 200 CE has enticed collectors worldwide. Glazed wares were first produced in the northeastern part of Thailand under Khmer control, from the 9th to the 13th centuries and subsequently at Sukhothai, Si Satchanalai and other kiln sites in central and northern Thailand. The most famous wares are celadons with incised designs, two glazed wares and wares with underglaze black decoration. The bodies of the wares produced at the Kalong kiln complex in the north are exceptionally fine thanks to the presence of kaolin in nearby areas. The best known Thai glazed ceramic design is that of a single fish at the centre produced in the Sukhothai and Si Satchanalai kilns. Production stopped after the destruction of Ayutthaya in 1767 but was reintroduced in the north during the late 19th century.

Textiles too have an ancient lineage. Hemp and cotton have been fabricated since around 700 BCE. Rock paintings of the prehistoric period abound throughout the land. Some idea of the painting can be gleaned from the 6th-century relief at Phra Phothisat Cave, Saraburi, somewhat later depictions of the Jataka on boundary markers at Muang Fa Daed, and from the late 13th century onwards incised and relief designs on Buddha Footprints. Ayutthaya period murals provide information about painting techniques and imported fabrics worn by

the court while 19th-century murals of northern Thailand give a delightful introduction to the culture and especially textiles of the area. Today's handwoven fabrics continue to attest to the creativity of the ancients, as do modern paintings.

The once great forests of Thailand must have provided timber for numerous types of woodcarvings in prehistoric times as well as the first millennium CE. Carved pediments on Ayutthaya period monastic buildings, manuscript cabinets, preaching chairs and pulpits give evidence of such a legacy. Happily woodcarving continues today as one of the most important crafts, particularly in the Chiang Mai area.

Opposite, below: A cross draft kiln of egg shape, Si Satchanalai, where one can still see the development of kilns from inground ones to kilns of this type. The egg-shaped kiln was developed at Jingdezhen, China, at the end of the Ming Dynasty.

Above left: Contemporary production of celadon ceramics, Mengrai Kilns, Chiang Mai.

Left: A Sukhotai underglaze iron painted fish plate, *ca* 14th–16th century.

Above : A wood carver expertly fashions an intricate design. Chiang Mai.

Buddha Images

As the centuries passed after the Buddha's *Parinirvana*, there was a movement among some Buddhists away from a closed Sangha community. Both monks and laymen turned towards a cosmology of merciful saints (Bodhisattvas). Central to this was the Buddha, originally only a revered human being, who now became a savior and deity. An icon thus was needed and in the 1st century CE an image of the new deity was created in the northwestern part of the Indian subcontinent.

Buddha images fashioned in what is now Thailand date from *circa* the 6th century CE and were created by the Mon people in central and northeastern Thailand. These images were greatly influenced in turn by Indian Gupta, Post Gupta and Pala Styles but the features of the images clearly resemble those of an ethnic group with strong indigenous attributes: large hair curls and faces, curved and connected eyebrows, prominent eyes, a broad nose and thick lips. Most Buddha images were carved of stone with smaller ones cast in bronze.

From the 11th to mid 13th centuries what is now Thailand was under the domination of the Khmer. A new type of image emerged; it had a square face divided into almost horizontal planes, straight eyebrows, hair usually topped by a cone shaped protuberance or a wide crown. If the latter, the body was usually decorated with necklaces, armlets, earrings and a jewelled belt.

In the mid to late 13th century Thais threw off the Khmer yoke. Images at first maintained Khmer characteristics but by the 15th century took on a totally Thai personality. The glory of Thai sculpture is the walking Buddha in the round. Those

Left: A bronze Sukhothai Buddha image with a flame finial above a slightly rounded *ushnisha* wears his *uttara-sanga* (robe) in the open mode with one end forming a fish-tail flap near the navel and his *sanghati* (shawl) in accordion pleats; his *antaravasaka* (undergarment) is seen at the waist through the transparency of the robe. Dated 1421 CE. Collection of Prince Rangsit.

Bottom left: A so-called late Chiang Saen Buddha image influenced by Sukhothai style images, *ca* late 15th to beginning of the 16th century (See Griswold 1957, Plate XXII).

Bottom middle: Buddha image from Kampaeng Phet, with a flame finial. The robe is worn in the closed mode covering both shoulders and the belting and median pleat of the undergarment appearing through it. *Ca* late 16th to the early 17th century. Private collection.

Below: Thailand's most famous Sukhothai walking Buddha image, with left hand in the *abhaya* mudra, *ca* 15th century. Height: 2.2m (6.8ft). (See Woodward 1999, 160 and Plate 162). Wat Benjamabophit, Bangkok.

dating to the early 15th century are a bit stiff, but a bit later they exhibit the supernatural anatomy of the Buddha given in the Sutras: the torso lion-like with broad shoulders, the arms, smooth and tapering and the heavy thighs resembling the stalks of a banana tree. In a supreme endeavour to capture the spirituality of the Buddha, no display of muscle or bone is apparent and the body under the thin robe is asexual. The Buddha's head is oval like an egg, his nose hooked like a parrot's beak, his chin rounded like a mango pit, the eyebrows arched over downcast eyes and a high flame finial indicative of his spiritual radiance.

At the same time the earliest dated seated Buddha images with a high flame finial were created in the Ayutthaya and Sukhothai Kingdoms. Later in the century and further to the north, in the Lan Na Kingdom, two styles of seated Buddha images were produced, one called the Lion-type or early Chiang Saen and another with a high finial like the images of Sukhothai and Ayutthaya known as late Chiang Saen. A B Griswold in his 1957 *Dated Buddha Images of Northern Siam* proved epigraphically that they were produced in the same period.

In 1438 Ayutthaya absorbed the Sukhothai Kingdom. Its increasing wealth and power is illustrated by the 16th- to 18th-century Buddha images; here the Buddha is represented as the universal ruler wearing the crown and royal regalia embellished with jewels of the Ayutthayan kings. This trend continued into the early Ratanakosin Era. In the mid 19th century King Rama IV commissioned Buddha images having no *ushnisha* and more human in nature. Later reigns restored the *ushnisha* but continued to represent the Buddha more naturally.

Above left: Lan Na Buddha image with a lotus finial high up on the *ushnisha*. That and the diadem with three small-prongs, one at the centre and one at each side, indicate a 16th-century date, probably *ca* early 16th century. Bangkok National Museum.

Above: Early Chiang Saen or lion-type Lan Na Buddha image, with large chest and curls and *ushnisha* topped by a lotus, seated with right hand in the *maravijaya* mudra, *ca* late 15th century. (For a virtually identical image see Griswold 1957, Plate XVI, dated 1490.) From the Royal Collection, Bangkok National Museum.

Left: Head of an Ayutthaya bronze image with thick band across the forehead, *ca* 14th to 15th century (see Woodward 1999, Plate 175). Collection of Phrakru Kanumsamanajam, Bangkok.

Below left: Bejewelled Buddha image in the regalia of an Ayutthaya king seated on a lotus base, *ca* 18th century. Bangkok National Museum.

Below right: Crowned Ayutthaya Buddha with filigree decorated diadem having flanges above the ears, *ca* 16th century. Height: 70cm (2.5ft). (See Woodward 1999. Plates 215, 220, 248). Private collection.

Far left: Crowned bronze Buddha image adorned with red and green enamel ornamentation, gems and pendants and both hands performing the *abhaya* mudra, an attitude interpreted in Thailand as "calming the ocean", a reference to the occasion when the Buddha prevented the Neranjara River from overflowing, *ca* early 19th century. Bangkok National Museum.

Left: The Buddha stands on a four-tiered lotus throne with both hands in the *abhaya* mudra and his robe in the covered mode. The crown, robe, shoes, throne as well as his hands are all heavily jewelled. The image is influenced by late Ayutthaya styles but dates to the early Ratanakosin period. Private collection.

Above left: A bronze Buddha image with *uttarasanga* in the closed mode covering both shoulders and the *antaravasaka* marked by the fold at the abdomen and the median pleat. Both hands seemingly are enlarged to emphasize the double *abhaya* mudra, *ca* late Ayutthaya. Private collection.

Above right: The future Buddha, Maitreya, seated in *prayankasana* on an imposing five-tiered lotus throne indicating he will be the fifth Buddha in this era. He wears a jewelled robe with floral patterns favoured on the robes of Buddhas and the monk Phra Malai in the early 19th century. Private collection.

Ayutthaya Painting

Thai murals are created on a background prepared and dried before the application of pigments mixed with glue. Thus they are not frescoes, which are painted on wet plaster. The technique was employed in the 11th–13th century murals of Pagan in neighboring Myanmar (Burma). One may surmise that Thailand too had murals of the type at that time.

As of the 17th century, saw-toothed bands were employed on the lower lateral walls of monastery buildings to separate the scenes from the Life of the Buddha, the Jataka (stories of the Buddha's 547 lives preparing for Buddhahood), as well as celestial figures in registers above them. The palette is restrained, limited to black, white, red and green with the main figures outlined in black. The paintings in general are two-dimensional although at times some of the buildings are depicted with a kind of perspective suggesting possible Western influence.

During the reign of King Borommakot (r 1733–1758) new designs were introduced as is evident from those at Wat Koh Keo Suttharam, Petchaburi. The Ayutthaya murals reached their apogee in the crypts at Wat Rajaburana, Ayutthaya, painted during his reign. These have been dated erroneously to 1424 because of an oblique reference in the *circa* 1680 Luang Prasoert Chronicle. However, the memoirs of King Uthumphon (r April–May 1758), who succeeded Borommakot, state that his father built Wat Rajaburana (Office of the Prime Minister 1991, 46). The murals affirm this for they show Sri Lankan influence from Borommakot's

Top: A golden pigeon and a long-beaked white bird probably indicate the Buddha's lives as birds during his 547 lives gaining merit, crypt of Wat Rajaburana, Ayutthaya. Reign of King Borommakot.

Above: Celestial beings paying respect to the relics of the Lord Buddha in a sacred urn, Wat Chomphuwek, Nonthaburi; *ca* late Ayutthaya period.

Opposite: A Brahma with hands in the gesture of adoration placed under a saw-toothed scene divider. He wears an elaborate golden crown, jewelry and imported fabric commensurate with his high status. Wat Yai Suwannaram, Petchaburi; *ca* beginning of the 18th century.

Left: The presiding Buddha image of Wat Koh Keo Suttharam, Petchaburi, echoes in style that of the meditating Buddha image in the mural to the rear being attacked by Mara's Army, which the earth goddess wrings water from her hair to disperse. On each side of the mural is a Buddha Footprint representing the Footprint on Adam's Peak and Phra Phuttha Bat. Dated 1734, early in the reign of King Borommakot.

Opposite, top left: Painting on wood of a rhinoceros perhaps suggesting that they were abundant in Thailand at the time, Sala Kan Parien, Wat Yai Suwannaram, Petchaburi; *ca* early 18th century.

Opposite, bottom left: A crowned celestial with flowing garments kneels in reverence, Wat Mai Prachum Phon, Ayutthaya. A *kamchiak*, an ornamental part of a crown suspended behind the ears, indicates an 18th-century date.

Opposite, far right: The figures of two celestial beings with their hands in the mudra of adoration depicted within an inverted triangle, the latter an important feature of the murals of Wat Koh Keo Suttharam, Petchaburi, 1734.

sending monks to that country to resuscitate Buddhism there and include a jewelled Footprint of the Buddha atop a mountain, indicating his devotion to the Footprint on top of Adam's Peak, Sri Lanka, and Phra Phuttha Bat on Mount Suvannapabbata, Saraburi, Thailand.

The murals first and foremost illustrate the Buddhist devotion of a nation made wealthy by trade and having foreigners in their midst. They depict a splendid court with kings and courtiers wearing intricately designed gold jewelry and elaborate crowns and headdresses as well as garments of the finest imported Indian textiles painted with designs ordered for court circles. The girdles with flying panels made from these cloths bring vibrancy to the murals, as do the saw-toothed dividers, the lines of which rise and fall in what often is a zigzag pattern.

Ratanakosin Painting

Ayutthaya artists were engaged in the building of Bangkok, the Ratanakosin capital, and basic painting themes were continued: On the East wall of the *ubosot* (ordination hall) facing the presiding Buddha is usually a depiction of the Buddha's Victory over Mara, on the West wall the Traiphum, the Buddhist cosmology of the Three Planes of Existence, and on the lateral walls either the Life of the Buddha or the Jataka or both with scenes placed consecutively between the windows which is the area most easily viewed by the faithful. Above, placed in registers, are worshipping celestials. While there was a tendency to recreate Ayutthaya, pride in the new city ensured innovations. To emphasize subjects artists began to paint them in light colours against a dark background. Blue now appeared frequently in the palette giving at times a brightness and at others a sobriety to the murals. The sawtoothed zigzag divider continued to be employed to separate scenes, but when two or more episodes were painted in one bay, the most important one was given a red background and the secondary green. Groves of trees were used at times to augment the zigzag dividers and emphasize scenes.

While King Rama II is well known for his mastery of the arts, it was mainly during the reign of his successor King Rama III that painting experienced remarkable developments. Artists followed the principles of traditional Thai art in their choice of themes, styles and basic techniques, but added numerous new ones, as at Wat Po, to provide an encyclopedic amount of knowledge to the public. Vignettes of local life

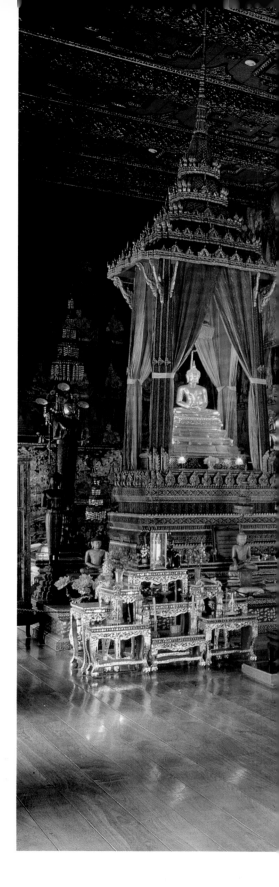

Right: Extensive murals in the Buddhaisawan Chapel, Palace of the Wang Na, built in 1795, now part of the Bangkok National Museum. Between the windows are scenes from the Life of the Buddha, above which celestial worshippers appear in four registers with beings having supernatural powers in the uppermost register. At the centre of the chapel is the much-revered image, Phra Buddha Sihing.

Above: Elements from nature complement the refined, elegantly dressed courtiers, the Buddhaisawan Chapel.

Left: A gold on black lacquer painting of the bamboo house and surroundings of the penniless Brahman, Jujaka, a vignette of local life, the Vessantara Jataka; *ca* The Third Reign.

Right: The chariots of King Sanjaya speed to the hermitage in the forest to bring Prince Vessantara and Maddi back to the capital, Vessantara Jataka. The depiction of the royal city is similar to that in murals in the Ordination Hall, Wat Suvannaram, Thonburi; *ca* the Third Reign. Painting on wood.

Both from the collection of Prince Rangsit.

became more prominent. As a result of increased trade with China an infatuation developed with Chinese art motifs, accompanied on the other hand by an interest in the many types of foreigners who had come to live in Thailand. They were at times represented in archaizing dress. Figures were often highlighted in gold against dark backgrounds. Although the zigzag dividers remained, their presence was reduced and much was made of landscape elements and foliage to separate scenes. The epics began at the lower part of the composition and moved toward the upper part, from an isometric projection to an aerial perspective.

When King Rama IV, who had educated himself in the sciences and civilization of the West, was the Abbott of Wat Bowornivet prior to his succession to the throne he brought about a great change in the direction in painting wherein a rationalistic ideal replaced the traditional themes. The murals at Wat Bowornivet are by the great monk painter Khrua In Khong: They depict scenes of contemporary life in Thailand side by side with images of Western countries. Inscriptions that show them to be morally edifying allegories accompany them. The paintings employ Western perspectives providing three dimensionality within a two dimensional medium. The introduction of these Western perspectives sparked a movement away from traditional Thai painting and opened the door to new forms.

Right: An orgy occurs at a theatrical performance during a funeral, the Ordination Hall, Wat Thong Thammachat, Thonburi; The Third Reign.

Opposite, top left: A painting showing women's dress during the reign of King Rama III. The women wear a sash across the shoulder to cover breasts that are depicted by circles, the Ordination Hall, Wat Suthat, Bangkok.

Opposite, bottom left: A painting on wood showing a Bodhisattva who is preaching to celestial beings; *ca* Reign of King Rama IV. Collection of Prince Rangsit.

Above: Painting on cloth of the Buddha's *Parinirvana*. Theatrical performances were given at funerals in the past. It has been theorized that such activities took place to conceal sadness; *ca* The Third Reign. Collection of Prince Rangsit.

Left: The Loi Krathong Festival, one of the 12 representations of the Royal Ceremonies of the Twelve Months, after Khrua In Khong. The Assembly Hall, Wat Rajapradit, founded in 1864 gives a faithful rendering of the buildings and the festival in Western perspective and thus constitutes a valuable record of life at that time.

Above: Mural depicting an allegory concerning the lotus in which a large lotus appears in a pond before persons in Western dress. By the monk painter Khrua In Kong, the first Thai to adopt the true three-dimensional perspective technique in Thai painting. The Ordination Hall, Wat Bowornivet, Bangkok. The Fourth Reign.

Lan Na Painting

Little is known about early Lan Na paintings. The basic technique employed in the extant murals is that of classical Pagan, Ayutthaya and the early Ratanakosin periods. However, there are indications that painting on wood may have been popular earlier as well. In Viharn Nam Tam, Wat Phra That Lampang Luang, Lampang, some painted wooden panels devoted to the Story of Indra attest to this theory. The designs of the palaces and the dress of the participants link the murals to those of the Tilawkaguru Cave Temple, Sagaing, dated to 1672, and other murals of the period in Myanmar (Burma). A classic scroll border of Persian derivation adds a significant touch. The main subjects of the extant Lan Na murals are the Life of the Buddha and the Jataka.

The murals on these pages date to around the third quarter of the 19th century during the Fifth Reign. The tales from the Jataka depicted, unlike those in Ayutthaya and Ratanakosin murals, represent non-canonical texts brought together in area. Lan Na murals lay great stress on the details of contemporary life and are not bound by stylizations found in the said murals. They are both less accomplished and less conventional, but are very sensitive in expression. Moreover, they give a picture of local textiles, customs, methods of transportation, architecture and especially worship — in short, everything that constitutes a particular culture. Burmese influence is very visible in the depiction of Buddha images, architecture and dress resulting from proximity and long earlier Burmese presence.

Above: Khatthana-Kumman's mother, wearing a traditional Nan skirt of wavy horizontal stripes and a Burmese type jacket and hair dress, carries lacquer baskets in typical local manner. Khatthana-Kumman Jataka, Viharn Charturamuk, Wat Phumin, Nan.

Right: The Buddha and his disciples loom large against a truncated forest and harsh mountain background in comparison to the carts, helpers with local shoulder bags and leg tattoos and livestock of Prince Khatthana-Kumman who appears to the right in royal costume highlighted by gold. Khatthana-Kumman Jataka, Viharn Charturamuk, Wat Phumin, Nan.

Left: The reclining Buddha listens to the heavenly musician Pancasika sent by the god Indra while below are scenes from the Candagadha Jataka depicting village life. Blue dominates while additions of red add cheer to the desolate countryside. Viharn, Wat Nong Bua, Nan.

Below left: Couples glimpsed through windows of a painted wooden house with triangular pediments. Viharn, Wat Buak Krok Luang, Chiang Mai.

Below right: A Thai Lue man leads a group of Thai Yai wearing their best colourful wraps to the palace where Nang Rochana awaits to select a future husband. A curious dog and the blue background heighten the viewer's interest. Viharn Lai Kham, Wat Phra Singh, Chiang Mai.

Opposite, top: Image of one of the four Buddhas who have appeared in this Buddhist era. Four such images placed back to back in the *viharn* indicates Burmese influence. Viharn, Wat Nong Bua, Nan.

Opposite, below: Servants wearing local Chiang Mai dress sleep in the palace as Prince Siddhartha takes leave of his wife and son. Viharn, Wat Buak Krok Luang, Chiang Mai.

The murals are in the Chiang Mai and Nan areas. In both sectors paintings bear some influence from Bangkok, as in the short headdress of the men. Also members of the court in Chiang Mai murals wear period cottons produced in Gujarat, Western India, for the Thai markets. There is other evidence of connections with foreign sources, such as in the design of the chandeliers in the Chiang Mai palace, which too appear in Bangkok and adjacent area murals and monasteries.

The palette consists of green, blue, black, yellow, orange, white and red with highlights in gold. Black is often heavily employed in Nan murals for outlining. During the reign of King Rama IV new saturated colours had become available from China and may explain the brightness of the colors. The murals are found in *viharn*, halls of general assembly and worship, rather than in ordination halls (*ubosot*), as is the case with paintings in monasteries to the south.

Temple Banners

From the Sukhothai period through the reign of King Rama VII (r 1925–1935) the *Phra-bot*, a painted banner on cloth which depicted a Buddha image, the Life of the Buddha or Jataka played an important role in Thai society. Banners were first painted by monks as objects of worship in the temple, but gradually the role of such banners changed. People later ordered them from painters and dedicated them to temples as a form of merit making for deceased relatives, or to pray for quick recovery from illness. Later, they dedicated banners to temples under their own names in the hope of gaining merit for themselves. Eventually, the popularity of banners moved to the home, where they were hung on the walls for worship and also to decorate the residences.

As the purpose of the banners changed over time, so did the size of the cloth and style of the paintings. Old banners were created on a large piece of cloth, approximately 2–3m long and 1–1.5m wide (6–10ft x 4ft). The size was gradually reduced to as small as 50cm x 50cm (20ins x 20ins).

The oldest extant banners, dating from the mid-Ayutthaya period to the beginning of the Ratanakosin period, depict a life-size Buddha standing alone or with his disciples. During the reign of King Rama III, the size of the Buddha and his disciples reduced to about three-quarters of the cloth. The remaining space was used for depicting scenes from the life of the Buddha or his ten last lives prior to enlightenment. During the time of Kings Rama IV and V, scenes of the life of the Buddha and the Jataka took up much more space until the

Above: The faithful pay their respects to a Buddha image that they have adorned with a long *tung*, a Northern Thai Buddhist banner, usually hung. Here the banner made of orange and gold paper has been wrapped around the image.

Left: *Phra-bot* with a painting of the Buddha, his left hand in the *abhaya* mudra, standing behind his disciples Mogallana and Sariputta, *ca* Reign of King Rama III.

Opposite, top left: The elderly Brahmin Jujaka follows his pretty young wife, carrying goods for her.

Opposite, top right: Brahmins from a neighbouring kingdom ask King Vessantara for his country's prized white elephant, which he gives them, thus infuriating the population. This forces his father to resume the kingship and send Prince Vessantara and his family into exile.

Opposite, bottom: Prince Vessantara, Maddi and their two children on their way to exile in the forest sit in a carriage drawn by four stags supplied by the gods after Vessantara had given away their four horses to four Brahmins.

All banners opposite courtesy of the Jim Thompson collection, *ca* Reign of King Rama VII.

entire piece of cloth was covered with them. One of the artists' favourite episodes was the return of the Buddha from Tavatimsa Heaven where he had given a sermon to his deceased mother. The more recent banners, created during the reign of King Rama VII, depicted only scenes from the Life of the Buddha or the Jataka, the favourite episode of which was the Vessantara Jataka. It depicts the culmination of the Buddha-to-be's striving for perfection as the Prince Vessantara who performs the greatest of acts of charity by giving away what is most precious, his children and wife, enabling him to be enlightened and become a Buddha.

Northern Thai Buddhist banners, or *tung*, are long and narrow and measure from 10cm to 40cm (4–16ins) in width and 1m to 5m (3–16ft) in length. They bear *khit* or *chok* (continuous or discontinuous) supplementary weft designs placed separately and vertically. The most popular designs are those of the *prasat* (palace or monument with a tiered palace-type roof) and elephants in parade. Through their creation the Tai Lue and Tai Yuan peoples of Northern Thailand honour the Buddha and at the same time provide a ladder to heaven for their ancestors, especially ones that may need a long ladder out of hell to heaven. *Tung* are used widely in temples and at ceremonies and festivals to which they add great colour and charm. They are made not only of woven cotton, which may include bamboo sections, but also of wood and of colourful paper.

Thai Manuscripts

Thai manuscripts are of two types, palm leaf and folded accordion pleated paper. The first is made of long thin palm leaves cut to size and dried after which a text is incised horizontally and darkened by soot. The completed leaves are numbered consecutively and tied by string in bundles through two holes pierced in the leaves. The palm leaf tradition derives from Indian prototypes dating from the 10th century or earlier and thus is an ancient tradition. Palm leaves were particularly employed in Thailand for the Buddhist canon and legends, astrological and herbal medicine texts, literature and poetry. Due to the small size of the palm leaf it was suited only for painted decoration on a small scale. Thus the larger *khoi* paper folding manuscript made from the fiber of the *Streblus asper* shrub was developed. The off-white paper was either inscribed with black ink and illustrated in conformity with the text or blackened with soot and inscribed in chalk.

Illustrated manuscripts are much sought after. The subjects most often illustrated are The Life of the Buddha and the Jataka, stories of the monk Phra Malai, Buddhist cosmology and the Ramayana. The earliest extant date to the 17th century.

Both types of manuscripts were carefully maintained and kept in manuscript boxes and chests often beautifully decorated (see pages 192–197). By the end of the 19th century influence from Europe had largely transformed and overwhelmed Thai painting styles. And with the advent of inexpensive book printing about the same time, the Thai manuscript tradition came to a virtual standstill.

Top: Lan Na palm leaf manuscript with gilded leaves encased between cinnabar lacquered wooden covers with decorative identifying markers. Courtesy of Neold, Bangkok.

Above: Kinnara and *kinnari*, mythical creatures half human and half bird in the Himavanta Forest, a scene from the Traihhumikatha (Cosmology of the Three Planes of Existence) on an illustrated *khoi* paper manuscript dated 1743 from Wat Sisa Krabeu, Thonburi.

Right: Illustrated *khoi* paper manuscript bearing figures of a crowned garuda and a *theppanom*, both with hands in the gesture of adoration, on each side of a Buddhist text. To the rear is a small gilt lacquer manuscript box and a larger chest with *theppanom* in a garden or forest. This is an adaption of the Ratanakosin *kammalo* style that depicts mythical beings in forest scenery.

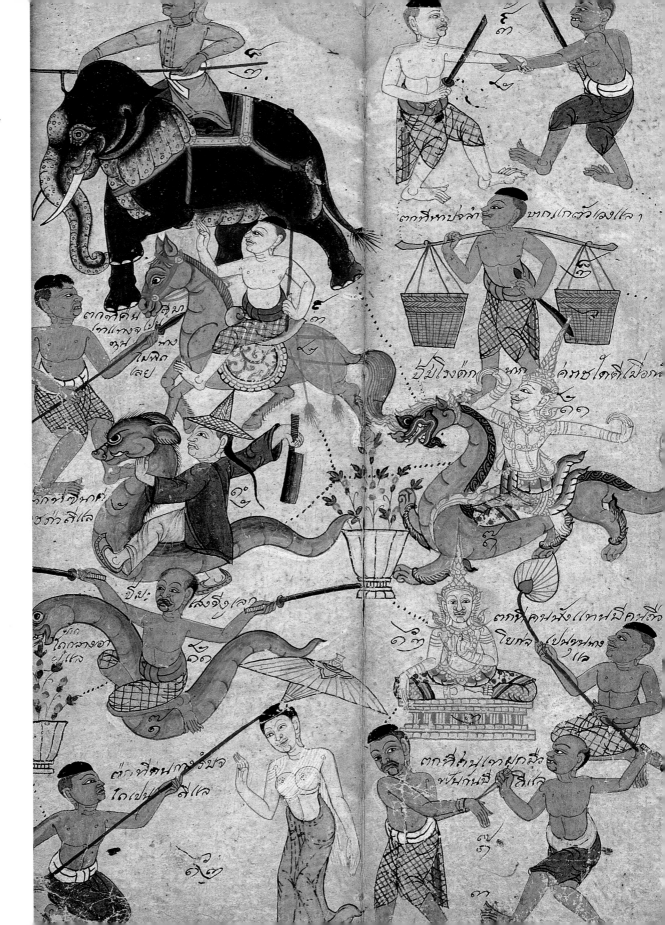

Right: An illustration from a fortune-telling manuscript in which a rich variety of figures that are 'character types' or 'mascots' such as a nobleman, swordsmen, an elephant mahout, a salesman carrying baskets of goods and various animals are shown. The system of fortune telling, based on the day and month of the birth date of the user, details the prospects for the client that are indicated by each mascot or group of mascots. *Ca* late 19th century when synthetic colours from Europe became available. Collection of William Warren, Bangkok.

Below: A Buddhist palm leaf manuscript wrapped in a waxed cloth to protect it from insects, tied with a cord and identified by an ivory marker.

Right: A manuscript devoted to the training of elephants shows the importance of the lasso and the elephant goad as instruments in controlling and teaching elephants. Reign of King Rama II.

ดาบโล่ห	ทหารอาชฯ และโล่ห	ดาบ และโล่ห
ซ้ายซ้าย	ขุนพล	ซ้ายขวา
ม้าซ้าย	ทับรอง	ม้าขวา
แซง	แซง	แซง

Opposite: An illustrated military strategy manuscript with the disposition of troops displayed against the body of a garuda whose fighting spirit is suggested by the flames of the *lai kanok*, a tripartite flame motif. 1815. Bangkok National Museum.

Right: Sketches depicting (top) the pursuit of a wild *gaur* (a type of ox) by hunters on elephant back; (middle) combat between an elephant and a tiger; (bottom) a mythical elephant lion-bird spewing and controlling elephant babies, the latter epitomizing the Thai love of the illusory. Late Ratanakosin period.

Far right, top: Manuscript showing a royal procession carrying new robes to present to monks at the end of the Buddhist Lent, after a mural at Wat Yom, Ayutthaya built in 1681 during the reign of King Narai the Great. 1897.

Far right, middle: One of the various types of prevalent cats documented in a manuscript devoted to cats and birds, Ratanakosin period, end of 19th to beginning of 20th century.

Far right, bottom: A royal procession by land and water, as in the reign of King Narai the Great. At the centre of each elaborately carved boat is a *busabok* used as a throne or to enclose a Buddha image or a relic. 1916. Collection of the National Library, The Fine Arts Department, Bangkok.

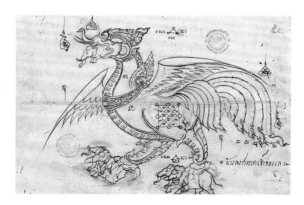

Right top: Two carved *tang* each with lion paw type feet. Courtesy of Neold, Bangkok.

Right middle: An intricately carved *tang* with unusual bird motif on the apron, legs and feet. Courtesy of Jim Thompson collection.

Right below: A lacquered and gilded carved 'wedding bed'; note the storage drawers under the canopy. To its left is a red and gold lacquered cabinet with tiered open shelves to place Buddha images. Rama II Memorial Museum.

Thai Furniture

The most versatile Thai furniture design is the *tang*, a square or rectangular seat raised on legs that comes in many sizes. When large, it serves as a bed or as a place to sit and entertain friends and dine. When small and of stool size, it often is stacked in pyramid fashion with several others of the same size to form a family altar. In former days women sat on a cushion in front of a *tang* upon which a mirror was placed to form a dressing table. The *tang* often has a lion paw or horsehoof shaped foot and is richly carved. When used for resting or sleeping it often had a polished bamboo or mat covering which added a cooling element to the surface. A *tang* appears as an auspicious symbol on a *circa* 14th-century Footprint of the Buddha found in Ayutthaya, indicating that its usage goes back a long time.

The base of the impressive canopy bed, sometimes called a 'wedding bed', is similar to a *tang* with a rectangular platform standing on four legs situated at the corner and walled in above by three low-back panels. A set of posts coupled with top braces are tenoned immediately inside the four outermost posts and it is upon this inner square frame that the lattice-work canopy rests.

A table used for dining is the *khantok*, a large round tray atop several pedestals attached to it with a round base. Presently the *khantok* is associated with Lan Na but an auspicious symbol on a *circa* mid 17th-century Footprint of the Buddha created in Ayutthaya indicates it once was popular in central Thailand.

As more foreigners came to live in the country in the 19th century, a small version of low bureaus/dressing tables were introduced as well as taller forms employed as altars for images.

Above: A large carved horse hoof footed *tang* seing new life as a modern sofa cum bed. Courtesy of Nagara Sambandaraksa.

Scripture Cabinets and Chests

Buddhist manuscripts when not in immediate use are kept in scripture cabinets and chests placed within a *hor trai* or scripture house. They may be tall and upright, of flat rectangular shape being both large and small, and of a shape particular to Lan Na with bodies wide at the top and diminishing in size below. Their donors provided the best materials and decoration that they could afford out of respect and to make merit.

The gilded lacquer decoration on such cabinets and chests was one of the most significant artistic mediums of the Ayutthaya and early Ratanakosin periods. It found its greatest expression in the employment of Thai motifs, which are imaginative transformations and adaptations of natural forms. One of the most important is the *kanok* motif, which is basically a vegetal one forming a right-angle triangle. Its distinctive feature is a flame-like contour. At times the motif may resemble both tongues of flame and climbing plants. The *kanok* often serves as a background for larger motifs such as Buddha images, *theppanom*, stupas, scenes from the life of the Buddha and the Ramakien. Within the motif often are animals and birds, some of which are mythical ones of the equally mythical Himaphan Forest. Such motifs do not appear only on scripture chests, cabinets and boxes, but frequently appear on window and door panels and other surfaces.

At times an intricate *kanok* design may be contrasted with one of another artistic medium as on late Ayutthaya scripture cabinets where a carved panel below strikes a contrast with the delicate intricate gilt patterns on the body panels.

Top: Carved and gilded panel from the bottom of a cabinet. At the center a *kirttimukha* spews two vines. On the right a winged European *putti* grasps the top vine. The design is similar to that of a carving on a scripture cabinet at the Somdet Phra Narai National Museum, Lopburi, dated by Listopad (1995, 309–311) to the 18th century prior to the fall of Ayutthaya. *Ca* the 18th century, prior to the fall of Ayutthaya, Wat Rakhang, Thonburi (for a full view of the cabinet, see page 8).

Above: A contrasting very delicate scene of two mythical beings frolicking within a forest of curly vegetation.

Right: A manuscript cabinet of a type known as 'pig's leg cabinet' with gilt on black lacquer designs depicting scenes including mythical beings in the Himavanta Forest and a seated Buddha. The latter may be the Lord Pacceka Buddha whom the Thai cosmological text *Traibhumikatha* says lives in that forest. A Pacceka Buddha is a Buddha who has achieved Enlightenment but does not teach. *Ca* 19th century. Jim Thompson Collection.

Above: A gilded lacquer chest with mythical lions, each bearing whorl designs on the body with the one to the rear plus the mane ending in a flame *kanok* motif. Their background employing the *phuttan* (cotton rose flower) motif suggests the chest dates to the reign of King Rama III who invented the motif for domestic and monastic architectural decoration. Bangkok National Museum.

Left: Two gilt lacquer manuscript boxes bear *theppanom* and other figures set against an elaborate *kanok* design. Of special interest is the *bai-sri* at the centre of the top box. This is a ceremonial structure of flowers and leaves often presented as a token of respect.

Above left: On a scripture cabinet panel two crowned and bejewelled *theppanom* stand stiffly as guardians amidst vertical and horizontal *kanok* motifs which provide life and lightness to the scene. *Ca* Ratanakosin period. The National Library, Bangkok.

Above right: In the early Ratanakosin period (Kings Rama I–III) the arts and crafts were still of Ayutthaya style although King Rama III introduced Chinese designs. The figures of a French noble and a Persian hearken back to the 17th-century reign of King Narai. An addition here to the *phuttan* and *kanok* motifs is the Thai curved line *ho* motif painted above the Persian, while above the French officer is a Chinese version of the *ho* motif. Bangkok National Museum.

Left: Nobles ride caparisoned horses against a backdrop of densely planted cotton rose bushes. The intricateness of the background plus the type of plants suggests the Third Reign period. The National Library, Bangkok.

Right: During the reign of King Rama III there was great interest in archaizing exoticism. In this scene from the Battle of Lanka in the Ramakien, European soldiers in the dress of the Ayutthaya period are placed within a Chinese architectural setting wherein dense Chinese type floral and cloud decoration takes the place of the classical *kanok* motif of the Ayutthaya period. *Ca* The Third Reign. The National Library, Bangkok.

Right: A cabinet of Chinese style decorated with Thai *theppanom* in gold on red lacquer popular in Lan Na, Chiang Mai National Museum, *ca* mid 20th century.

Top left: A *chedi*, ceremonial fans and banners decorate the centre of a high lacquered manuscript cabinet. It is wide at the top and narrows to the base in Burmese style but the designs indicate it was made in Lan Na. Museum, Wat Phra Keo Don Tau, Lampang; *ca* 19th century.

Left: A *theppanom* with hands in the mudra of adoration sits within an entwining floral scroll within yet another floral scroll. Gold on black lacquer against gold on red lacquer background; Museum, Wat Phra Keo Don Tau, Lampang; *ca* 19th century.

Preaching Chairs

Over the centuries, a variety of *thammat* or preaching chairs for monks and Abbots were made in Thailand. The oldest form is the *thammat thaen* or *tiang*, a rectangular seat without a back panel supported on straight or lion-shaped legs. This is still in use in rural areas. Somewhat later came the *thammat tang* of *chaise longue* shape.

In the Ayutthaya period the *busabok thammat* and *sangkhet* developed. The former is a throne set high on a tiered base, having pillars at each corner, with a canopy (*busabok*) above. This canopy takes the form initially of a tiered roof known as a *mondop* roof. Above it is a mound and then a finial. The tiers of the *busabok*'s *mondop* roof and the mound above represent Mt Meru and its surrounding mountains at the center of the Buddhist universe. This and the *thammat* suggest the Human Realm. Immediately above Mt Meru and indicated by the finial are the Six Deva Realms and above those the 16 Realms of Brahmas with Form. The Buddhist monks and members of their congregation familiar with these hierarchical aspects of Buddhist cosmology would recognize them in the *busabok thammat*. In turn those experienced in Jhanic, also called Dhyani, meditation would correlate their meditative progress with these hierarchical realms as they reached higher and higher realms themselves.

The *sangkhet*, however, was made for chanting by a group of monks. It consists of a wide horizontal seat, again raised on a platform and covered with a tiered roof. *Krachang*, lotus bud-like motifs, were used for border decoration to give a sense of

Top: Thammat tang with *singh* (lion)-paw feet and elaborate carvings. Courtesy of Neold, Bangkok.

Above: Figures with hands raised in the gesture of adoration on the preaching seat of the *busabok thammat* now at Wat Pho Puek, Ayutthaya. Below are two rows of *krachang* motifs and then floral motifs inset with cut glass of various colours. *Ca* early 17th century.

Left: Carved and gilded preaching chair on a pedestal platform with a footstool, all with lion-paw type feet. The chair is decorated at each side with a lotus bud of *krachang patiyan* design. The back support bears a striking gild design on black lacquer. In front of it is the Abbot of the monastery's embroidered silk cushion and to the side his fan. Wat Rakhang, Thonburi. *Ca* Ratanakosin period.

Above: Stairs with *naga* motif to mount a *busabok thammat*.

Above right: Busabok *thammat*, Wat Choengtha, Ayutthaya. Note in the roof the mound with tiers below indicating Mt Meru and the Human Realm and the finial above suggesting the Deva and Brahma Realms. *Ca* late Ayutthaya period.

Right: A step in the form of a goat with open wounds, perhaps to remind one of being reborn an animal if one does not make merit.

Opposite, left: Sangkhet, Wat Choengtha, Ayutthaya, with the lines of *krachang* motif. *Ca* late Ayutthaya period.

Opposite, right: Carved and gilded *busabok thammat* from Wat Mani Chonkan, Lopburi, bearing an inscription dating it to 1682 during the reign of King Narai the Great. Now in the Somdet Phra Narai Niwet Museum, Lopburi.

rhythmic pattern. The areas under the roofs of the *busabok thammat* and *sangkhet* bore designs as well. All were wooden and decorated with cut coloured glass, lacquer and gilding.

Ratanakosin period *thammat* followed strict design conventions and were influenced by later Ayutthaya styles, though some details were changed. Roofs had three to five tiers. Pillars having 12 redented corners and decorative motifs were introduced. The carving became shallower and the motifs more slender. The base, however, was higher and elaborately decorated. Lacquer, gilding, coloured cut glass and carving continued to be used extensively.

Lan Na Pulpits

Lan Na pulpits — also known as *thammat*, and wooden — have a striking individuality with more freedom of expression than those of central Thailand. They do, however, include various motifs found on the latter, especially the *kanok*, *krachang* and *naga*, albeit at times with greater movement. Most are no more than 200 years old.

The *busabok thammat* has a high and often waisted base. The seat is enclosed with a high partition at the centre of each side and several pillars at each corner. Its roof rises in tiers at each cardinal point of which is a carved or lacquer decorated triangular *na ban* (gable) bordered by finials, at the top a *cho fa*, at the sides *bai raka* and at the bottom *hang hong* (see right).

A second type of *thammat* is radically different with no pillars on the side and tiers above. Instead it is a dramatic wooden box-like pulpit with the top open at a height level with that of the seated monk delivering the sermon. It is mostly angular in shape with either four or six sides, one of which is open to allow access. This type of pulpit is placed high on what may be a base of separate material.

A third style is a *thammat* with a canopied roof and (usually) a long rectangular body. It is believed to have been modeled on the funeral bier used for nobility. There is also a fourth *thammat*, similar in form to the third in style but with a narrower body. Called *asana*, it is used as a seat for monks during a sermon and to hold various ceremonial requisites. As with the pulpits of Central Thailand that have roofs, the area below the roof may be carefully decorated.

Above: Teak *busabok thammat* with typical high waisted base, preaching seat enclosed by pillars and covered by a tiered roof with a gable at the center of each tier side. *Ca* latter half of the 19th century. Wat Phra Keo Don Tao, Lampang.

Right: A Buddha image in the Victory over Mara gesture gazes at a *busabok thammat* with gilt designs on red and black lacquer and tiers decorated with the gable at each cardinal point bordered by finials, a *cho fa* at the top, *bai raka* on the sides and *hang hong* at the base. *Ca* 3rd quarter of the 19th century. Viharn Chaturamuk, Wat Phumin, Nan.

Right: Black lacquered wooden open top scalloped-edged four-sided *thammat* with a large gilt *krachang patiyan* design at the centre of each side and a waisted cement pedestal base adorned with lotus blossoms and petals inlaid in stucco. Viharn Phra Nang Chamathevi, Wat Pong Yang Khok, Hang Chat District, Lampang. *Ca* early to mid 19th century.

Top, left and right: Lacquered and gilded flowerpots with stylized lotus blossoms carved in relief on the front and rear sides of a wooden pulpit dated 1751. Main *viharn*, Wat Phra That Lampang Luang, Lampang.

Above right: Bird with a tail of *kanok* vegetal design, flowers of *dok phuttan* (cotton rose flower) design, and other flowers with a Lan Na *dok tan tawan* (sunflower) design, in gold on black lacquer. *Ca* 2nd quarter of the 19th century or a little later.

Above left: Panel with gilt Chinese *dok phuttan* design on vermilion lacquer above and gilt on black lacquer below with a carved relief border of a *krachang ta oi* (sugar cane eye) design. *Ca* 2nd quarter of the 19th century or a little later since the *dok phuttan* design was introduced in the 2nd quarter of the 19th century.

Both in the Wat Phra Keo Don Tao Museum, Lampang.

Left: Asana for four monks with the upper section bearing the maze-like Chinese design *prachae chin* while the lower panels are carved with a *kankhot* motif. Gold leaf and inlaid glass decorates cinnabar and black lacquer, dated 1855. Main *viharn*, Wat Phra That Lampang Luang, Lampang.

Left below: Boldly designed golden lotus seed heads on black lacquer contrast with the delicate blue, black and gold floral motifs decorating a gilt and cinnabar background on the under side of the roof of the above *asana.*

Opposite: Open top waisted pulpit with gilt on vermilion lacquer panel and much applied relief-moulded gilt lacquer with glass inlay suggesting Burmese influence. Note the exceptionally curvaceous pulpit steps to the rear. *Ca* mid 19th century. *Viharn,* Wat Lai Hin, Lampang.

Ceremonial Containers

Ceremonies — especially Buddhist and royal — play a large role in Thai society, so there are ceremonial containers of many shapes and materials in use. Gold, silver, copper, brass, lacquer and wood are often employed. Amongst the most expensive and impressive are the neilloware ceremonial containers.

Neilloware, or *krueng thom,* was introduced to Thailand in the early Ayutthaya period and soon became associated with Nakorn Si Thammarat where it is still being made. A popular art form, it takes its name from the Italian word *niello,* meaning 'black'. Neillo is a combination of a non-metallic compound of sulphur and an alloy of silver, copper and lead that when rich in sulphur becomes a glossy black. The product is ground into a powder, which is then suspended in water and brushed on a metal. For fine pieces, silver is used. The black surface may be carved to expose the silver or gold may be employed to form a design on the blackened surface to which enamelling may be added. According to historical records neilloware was used only by kings, the royal family or noblemen of high rank. Thai kings used gold neillo items — offering containers, incense holders, and candlesticks — in religious ceremonies. Common vessels used in daily life included gold-neillo water bowls with a *phan* (a pedestal tray), storage pots and betel sets.

In the past every house had a betel set, often erroneously called a betel nut set, so they could make betel quids for guests. Each set contained a lime container and spreader, an areca nut cutter, a mortar and pestle to crush the areca nut and betel leaf holders. These in turn were placed on trays of a betel box.

Top: Enamelled gold neillo *khan dok,* a vessel with a high pedestal base used to hold flowers during religious ceremonies in the North and Northeast (on left). Enamel decorated gold neillo *phan wenfaa,* ceremonial set of one pedestal tray atop a larger one (on right). Courtesy of Neold, Bangkok.

Above: A *phan,* a pedestal tray, holds a large repoussée *sa-loong,* a Northern Thai term for a large silver bowl regarded as a status symbol, plus smaller bowls of the same design. Courtesy of the Nagi Shop, Bangkok.

Above: Two silver pedestal based bowls, both of which were created from alternating lotus petals and stamens designs, with the petals in the larger engraved with *kanok* motifs. Courtesy of the Nagi Shop, Bangkok.

Left: Pedestal trays and large bowl, covered box and rectangular tray atop a low table, all of mother-of-pearl inlaid in black lacquer. Courtesy of Neold, Bangkok.

Above: Gold niello pedestal tray with large bowl, a small bowl, kettle and a pedestal tray bearing a betel set including a tall lime pot, an octagonal box and a rectangular betel box. The latter was introduced during the reign of King Rama IV. Private collection.

Top left: A Northern Thai style betel set with 5 silver utensils: a betel leaf holder, an open container for chopped areca nuts and 3 other containers for ingredients, within a lacquer betel box. To the side is a horn of plenty betel leaf holder used in Northern Thailand and Laos. The Nagi Shop, Bangkok.

Top right: Gold niello tray and cosmetic containers with conical multi-tiered lids. Private collection.

Bottom left: Silver betel set containers of oval and circular shape from the North and a lime pot with spreader from Central Thailand. Also from The Nagi Shop, Bangkok.

Bottom right: Gold neilloware miniature betel set on a tray with storage drawer. To the rear is a gold and enamel encrusted nielloware box. Bangkok National Museum. All the above date to the Ratanakosin period.

Right top: Si Satchanalai celadon dish with incised lotus blossoms and petals in the well and a single lotus blossom at the centre. *Ca* 15th century.

Right below: Si Satchanalai underglaze iron-decorated dish with a classic scroll design on the rim, floral plants on the well and a blossom at the centre. *Ca* late 15th to early 16th century.

Thai Ceramics

In the latter part of the 13th century ceramic production moved from northeastern Thailand to areas associated with the emerging kingdoms — to Suphanburi in west-central and to Sukhothai and Si Satchanalai in north-central Thailand and Phan, Kalong and San Kamphaeng and other sites in the Lan Na. It is not certain when production in Lan Na began, but recent findings on the shipwreck Turiang, dated tentatively 1305–70, reveal that the kilns in the three said central areas were producing at that time. Wares with underglaze iron designs were introduced, as were celadon and brown wares and later white, and white and brown. Generally, the wares follow Chinese ones, but the materials, interpretations of designs and introduction of new motifs sets them apart as Thai.

The most distinctive motif is that of a single fish created with a few brush strokes. Floral designs, especially the lotus, were both painted and incised at the centre and in the well of dishes and bowls. It and the *cakkavudha* (discus), the latter in the form of a spiralling flower head, are auspicious Buddhist symbols. Animals, elephants at work and war, in particular, were skillfully fashioned. The movement and the power of the bat designs painted on Kalong dishes are rivalled by few in the ceramic world.

For a long time scholars thought the wares dated from the 14th to the mid 16th century when the kilns were destroyed by war. Recently, evidence from shipwrecks and comparisons with Chinese wares have provided information that Thai kilns resumed production after the war.

Right: Si Satchanalai two-color glaze baluster vase with a body bearing incised floral scrolls within lotus frames. The form of the baluster vase derives from Kangxi China (1662–1722) but its decoration is Thai.

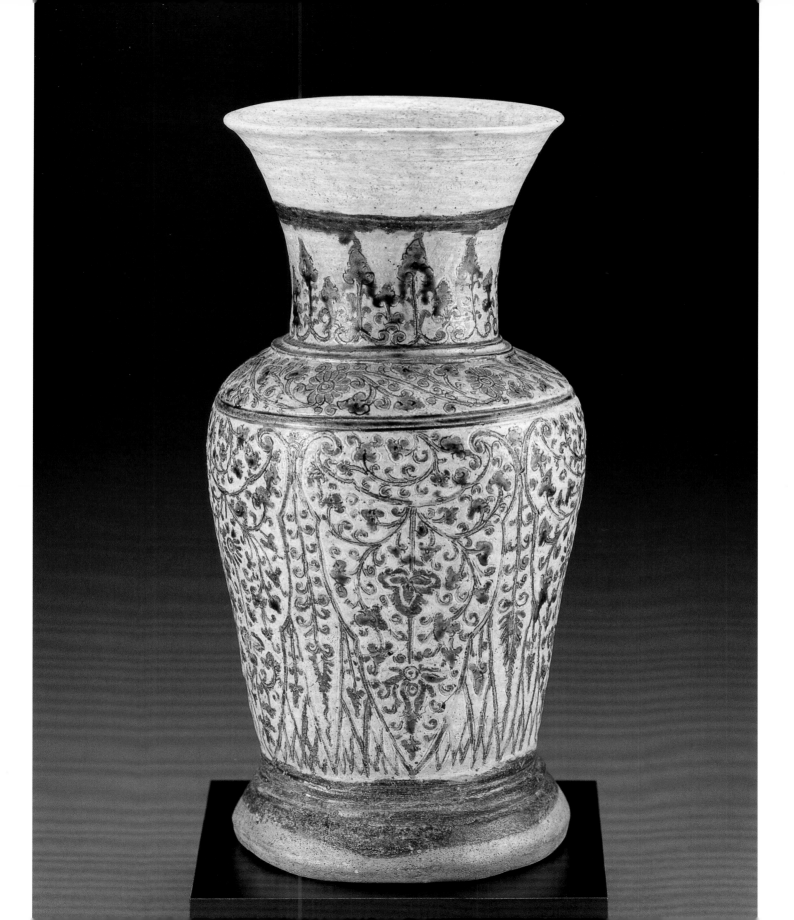

Above: Two-colour glazed architectural ornament from Si Satchanalai in the form of a three-headed *naga. Ca* 17th to 18th century.

Above right: Two-colour glazed Si Satchanalai figure of a *yaksa* (ogre converted to the service of Buddhism) wearing a crown similar to those of 17th-century crowned Buddha images.

Right: Si Satchanalai two-colour glazed figure of a *theppanom* with 17th-century type crown.

Right: Si Satchanalai underglaze iron decorated covered
jars and water dropper with
alternating diaper and vegetal
sprays. *Ca* late 16th to early
17th century.

Right below: Sukhothai bowls
with underglaze iron decorated fish at the centre and
vegetal forms in the well.
Bowls bearing this design
were found on the shipwreck
Rua Si Chang II dated 1577.

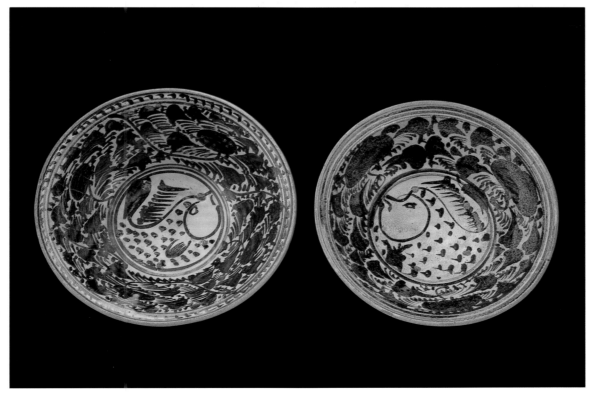

Opposite: Si Satchanalai celadon figure of a man holding what may be his prize fighting cock.

Top left: Si Satchanalai two-colour water dropper in the form of a mandarin duck. *Ca* 15th century.

Top middle and right: Si Satchanalai water dropper of a man holding a pot. He and a figure holding a cock both have a plug of fermented tea popular in the area and to the north in their left cheek.

Right: Si Satchanalai figurines reflecting the local importance placed on animals and the life of the people.

The figurines may date to the late 16th to early 17th century since many of the type were found on the Ao-Thai shipwreck of that period.

Right: Kalong kiln pear-shaped bottle with flanged neck and underglaze iron vegetal design. The shape derives from Chinese bottles of the late 17th to early 18th century.

Below: Yuan Dynasty shaped San Kamphaeng stoneware jar with two lugs in the form of dragons influenced by wares created during the reign of Emperor Yongzheng (r 1723–1735). The employment of ancient shapes and designs was popular in Qing Dynasty China and copied in Thailand.

Opposite, top left: Kalong underglaze iron decorated dish with spiralling leaves at the centre and a wide band in the well of such leaves, influenced by Qing dynasty *famille verte* designs. *Ca* late 17th to early 18th century.

Opposite, top right: Kalong dish decorated with an underglaze bat motif, influenced by a bat motif introduced in the reign of Emperor Yongzheng.

Opposite, below left: Kalong underglaze iron decorated dish with bat and floral motifs. *Ca* 1723–1735.

Opposite, below right: San Kamphaeng dish with underglaze iron two-fish motif at the center, a Song Dynasty motif re-introduced to China in the early 18th century and mentioned in a 1729 imperial kiln list.

Thai Textiles

Textile production in Thailand has been traced back to prehistoric times, but the art of weaving still flourishes today. Remains of fabric impressions on bronze and iron artefacts show coarse and open plain weave, mostly comprised of unequal warp and weft. The fibres have been identified as hemp and cotton, with the majority hemp. More recently, the two most employed fibres were cotton and silk. Cottons lend themselves well to indigo, black, cream and red-brown dyes, while silks were predominantly dyed red, yellow and green to suit the acidity of the fibre. The palettes radically changed with the introduction of pinks, purples, turquoise and blue from aniline dyes in the late 19th century.

Certain designs found on textiles can be traced back to the Dong-son bronze culture (500 BCE–100 CE) that extended to what is now Thailand. These, considered as power symbols, include angular meanders, hooks, spirals, eight-pointed stars, scrolls, elephants, birds and spirit figures.

Later, another major influence was the silk *patola*, which originated in Gujarat, India, and was traded in Thailand from the 15th century. A long double ikat resist-dyed cloth, measuring up to 4m (13ft), it has a central field decorated with various motifs, decorative borders along both selvedges and triangular motifs at each end of the fabric. As the Ayutthaya Kingdom became more powerful these were ordered in large numbers for the court: They were worn as *pha chong kra ben*, the material being wrapped and tucked around the body to create a pantaloon-style garment for men, and also in *na nang* style

All textiles here and following pages from the Paothong Thongchua Collection.

Above: Gold painted textile for royalty, used especially for cremations, 180–200 years old.

Right: Cloth for a court Brahman, 150–180 years old, Rama III period, from Nakorn Si Thammarat which at one time was famous for *pha yok*, delicate, gold patterned textiles created by metallic and coloured continuous supplementary weft yarns (*khit*) using silk from the Northeast and local cotton.

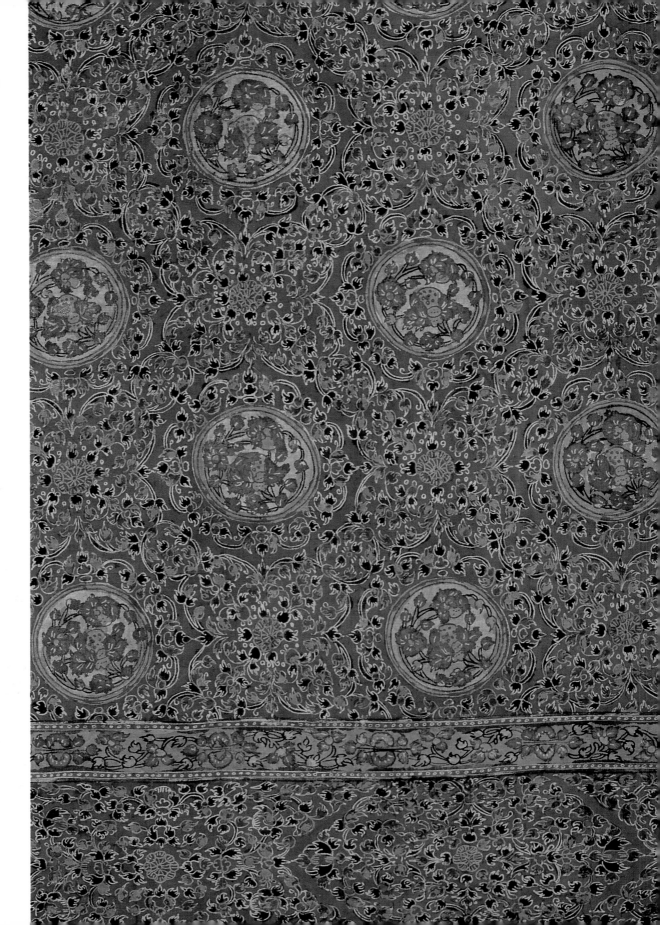

Right: Indian cotton textile with a floral pattern featuring rondels within frames. It may have been used as a hanging or it could have been a *pha nung,* or ceremonial skirt-cloth; 150–200 years old.

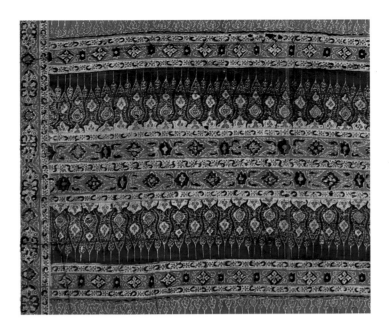

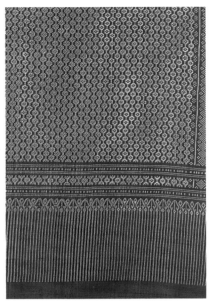

for the women, with the material wrapped around the body and pleated at the front. As time went by the *patola* were embellished with brocades (interwoven raised designs), metallic threads and jewels. Ayutthaya sumptuary laws accorded only the king and queen the wearing of gold brocaded satins, while other consorts wore less elaborate brocades. Wives of ministers and royal servants were dressed in graded qualities of fabric according to rank. Orders were sent for *patolas* bearing Thai motifs. At the same time fabrics hand painted and printed with wooden blocks and resist-dye techniques were imported.

Thais unable to afford such imported luxury goods began to make local copies in cotton and silk. They developed an affinity for weft ikat; indeed, the Thai name for ikat is *mat mii*, which is associated with weft ikat rather than double or warp ikat. *Mat mii* is a resist-dye technique whereby the yarns of the weft are tied with water resistant strings to resist the dye and thus create a pattern in the weft yarns before they are woven. Designs employing *mat mii* have played a large role in the *pha sin*, a tubular skirt worn by women outside the court. This skirt width is such that it is larger than the body of the wearier. The access is folded either to the left or right in such a manner that it forms a straight line from the waist to the bottom. The uppermost part of this fold is tucked into the waist to tightly secure the skirt from falling and an ornamental metallic belt may be added. The *pha sin* is composed of three parts: the waist band, the body and the hem. The three parts may be woven all in one or may be woven separately and then

Above left: Painted ceremonial cotton skirt-length from India's Coromandel Coast for the Thai trade, comparable in quality of colour and delicacy of drawing to the best chintzes exported to Europe. *Ca* late 18th century.

Above middle: Nakorn Si Thammarat gold brocade on purple silk; 80–100 years old.

Above right: An 1890 photo of a prince wearing a brocaded *pha chong kra ben* and some splendid jewelry.

Above: Mural of women in the costume of the Rama IV period wearing printed fabrics and sashes of various colours and motifs placed around the bust and draped over one shoulder. Wat Rachapradit, Bangkok.

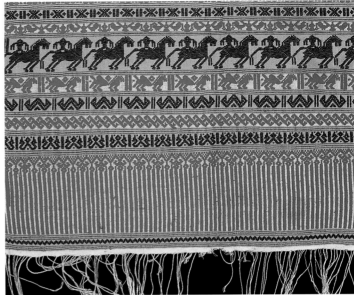

attached. The latter structure makes more possible the use of expensive yarns in the body and more durable ones in the waist and hem. It also makes possible the addition of a specially woven hem piece called in Thai *tiin*. Plaids have often been used for men's garments: these include the *pha* sarong, the male lower garment and the men's *pha khaaw maa*, a multipurpose cloth used as a sash, carrying sling or shoulder wrap.

Around the middle of the 19th century, courts in Thailand banned the importation of Indian fabrics as the Thais had begun to take pride in local production of weft *mat mii*, continuous and discontinuous supplementary weft with metallic threads and of brocades. This is readily seen in extant fabrics woven in Nakorn Si Thammarat and Chiang Mai.

Weaving was women's work. They not only wove clothes for the family and textiles for household use, but also produced textiles to be used in the service of Buddhism. Other textiles included banners, handkerchiefs and towels, bedding, pillows for sitting and resting, monks' shoulder bags, fans, manuscript covers and long rolls of cloth on which were painted the story of the Vessantara Jataka to accompany the ceremony devoted to its preaching. Mothers took great pride in the weaving of special clothing for their sons' ordination into Buddhism, such as the *pha pok bua*, the headcloth of a novice going to ordination.

Thai textiles are woven by many Thai groups. While the *mat mii* technique has been very popular, other techniques have been used in the weaving of Thai fabrics and treated differently by the various groups as is noted on these pages.

Top left: A pillow woven by a member of the Lao Phuan, a group originally from Northeastern Laos, whereon bright supplementary yarns have been employed to produce angular and geometric forms plus ones of an amorphous nature, suggesting a carry over of ancient designs. 80–100 years old. From Lopburi.

Above: Two Lao Phuan ladies' scarves decorated with continuous supplementary weft (*khit*) and discontinuous supplementary weft (*chok*) yarns forming zoomorphic patterns.

Left: Lao Phuan *pha sin* from Hat Seao, 10 km (7 miles) north of Si Satachanalai. 100–120 years old.

Below: Late 19th-century mural at Wat Phumin, Nan, shows a lady wearing a sash which covers the front of her neck and flows to her back. In the period women only covered their breasts when going to the *wat*. Her *pha sin* bears a famous Nan horizontal pattern called *lai naam lai* (flowing water).

Bottom: Carved wooden loom shaft pulleys, each with a horse at the top. Jim Thompson Collection, Bangkok.

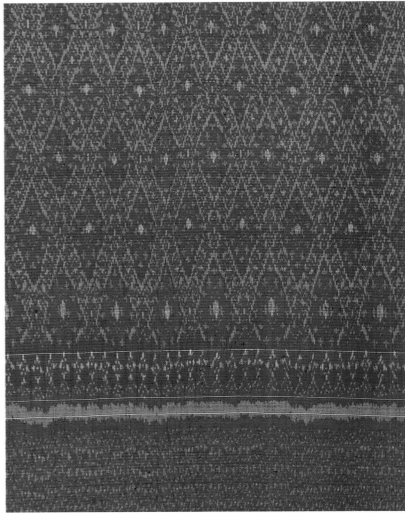

Above: Lady's rare double ikat *pha sin*, 80–100 years old. Surin, northeast Thailand.

Top right: Lady's weft *mat mii pha sin*, with a distinctive diamond pattern on the body, 80–100 years old. Surin.

Right: Thai spinning wheel and skein-winder, the latter in the form of a composite being, an alligator with an additional *naga* (serpent) head. Jim Thompson Collection, Bangkok

Above: A check and a plaid for men. The latter contains a silk warp and two-colour plied yarns in the weft. These plied yarns, called *hang karauk*, (literally 'squirrel's tails') are twisted and create a shimmering plaid. Both 80–100 years old and from Surin.

Left: Thai soldiers on parade wear *pha chong kra ben* which are mostly plaid. Above they wear for the most part floral *pha khaaw maa*. From a 1897 manuscript after the murals at Wat Yom, Ayutthaya, built in 1681. The National Library, Bangkok.

Left: Silk *pha sin* with *tiin chok*, ie a border with discontinuous supplementary weft decoration, here of silk, silver and gold threads, with a lozenge motif at the centre. 130–150 years old. From Chiang Mai.

Below: Princess Ubon Wanna, daughter of King Kawilorot Suriyawong (1856–1870), Chiang Mai, wears a *pha sin tiin chok* as do her attendants.

Bottom: Pha sin of silk, gold and silver thread with horizontal geometric patterns in the body and the *tiin chok* with a lozenge motif at the centre. 130–150 years old. From Chiang Mai.

Below and right: Thai Lue in Nan, Chiang Kham, Phayao Province, Chiang Khong and Chiang Rai weave *pha sin* employing the *ko* or *luang* technique, a tapestry technique whereby different coloured weft yarns are woven like plain weave, but hook and dove-tail together around the warp yarns to ensure a strong bond in the fabric. This is evident in the centre of the bodies of these two *pha sin* from Chiang Rai Province. 60–80 years old.

Left: A Lao Kram *pha sin* with body bearing alternating bands of weft *mat mii* and continuous supplementary weft, the fabric of the body having been woven with a horizontal pattern which was then placed vertically when the body was created. A *tiin chok* border with a design of large lozenges at the center is attached to it. 80–100 years old. From Chainat Province.

Below: Monk's bag woven by a Tha Yuan who migrated from Chiang Saen in the north to Ku Bua near Rachaburi in Central Thailand. 80–100 years old.

Opposite: Thai Yuan *pha pok bua*, a headcloth used by a novice prior to ordination, in plain weave with discontinuous supplementary weave. 80–100 years old.

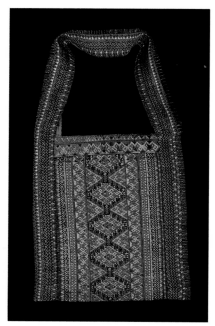

Gold and Silver Jewelry

Gold jewelry enhanced by gems has been popular in Thailand since the middle of the first millennium. Local artisans employed repousée, granulation and filigree techniques in addition to the Indian *kundan* method of setting a gemstone in gold by using bands of almost pure gold. The latter eliminates the need for fabricating a bezel, a gemstone-setting frame for each stone used, and allows a large number of irregular and uncut stones to be included in a setting. Extant antique Thai jewelry indicates that stone quality and regularity of cut, though not totally ignored, was of lesser importance than the general effect of created glitter and opulence. Jewelry was meant to indicate rank and wealth.

Thus jewelry was — and still is — lavished with cabochons and table-cut gems. Often enamelling was applied to heighten the gold patterns. Previously, enamelling had been raised to an art form in Moghul India and is believed to have been practised in Thailand since the reign of King Ekatosarot (r 1605–1611). Initially, only red and green enamels were used, but as the materials became scarcer other colours such as blue, deep blue and white were added and is very evident in Ratanakosin period jewelry.

An important design is the *noppa-ratana* or nine gems. This derives from ancient Hindu cosmology as reflected in *nava-rattana* settings whereby nine gems symbolize the nine planets. Such settings formed a powerful amulet by polarizing all space in relation to the sun, the giver of life, and mankind in relation to the universe. The gemstones, either together or

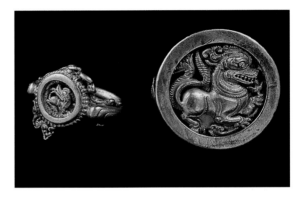

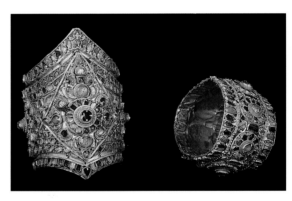

Right: Necklace composed of gold cylinders and beads with attached pendants having a large central gem plus smaller ones and enamelling. Ayutthaya period, *ca* 17th to 18th century.

Above top: A pendant with a *noppa-ratana* type gemstone setting of cabochons at the center consisting of eight gems encircling a central grouping and enhanced by an enamelled background. *Ca* late Ayutthaya period.

Above middle: Ring with an embossed mythical lion. *Ca* 17th century.

Above bottom: Gold armlet and bracelet from the crypt, Wat Rajaburana, Ayutthaya, decorated with rubies. The armlet has at each cardinal point a *noppa-ratana* setting consisting of eight cabochons around yet another gemstone setting at the centre which represents the ninth gem of the *noppa-ratana*. *Ca* late Ayutthaya period. Ayutthaya National Museum.

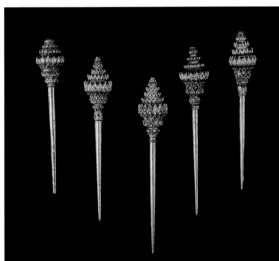

Above, clockwise from top left: Gold ear studs with s-shaped hook, late 19th and early 20th century. Necklace with unusual fish pendants in addition to the central one. Late Ayutthaya period. Gold hairpins decorated with variously coloured enamels. *Ca* 19th century.

Opposite: Silver purse of braided tiny silver strips, embossed and engraved bracelets, buckles with embossed designs and belts of coiled and chain wire. Northern Thailand, early to mid 20th century. Courtesy of the Nagi Shop, Bangkok.

separately, were used for preventative, therapeutic and anti-dotal purposes. The latter concept was adopted by the Moghul rulers of India whose magnificent jewelry in turn influenced that of Ayutthaya. For the most part, Ratanakosin jewelry maintained the traditional designs and production techniques but the settings were more detailed.

Nicholas Gervaise, the French priest who lived in Ayutthaya in the late 17th century, mentioned the thousand styles of beautiful, delicate silver ornaments with silver so delicately inlaid into the surface of the ornaments that it was difficult to see the connection. Sadly, however, there is no extant silver jewelry earlier than a century old. Nakorn Si Thammarat, Bangkok and Chiang Mai have been closely associated with the production of silver in the Ratanakosin period while Petchaburi has become the Thai centre for traditional style gold jewelry.

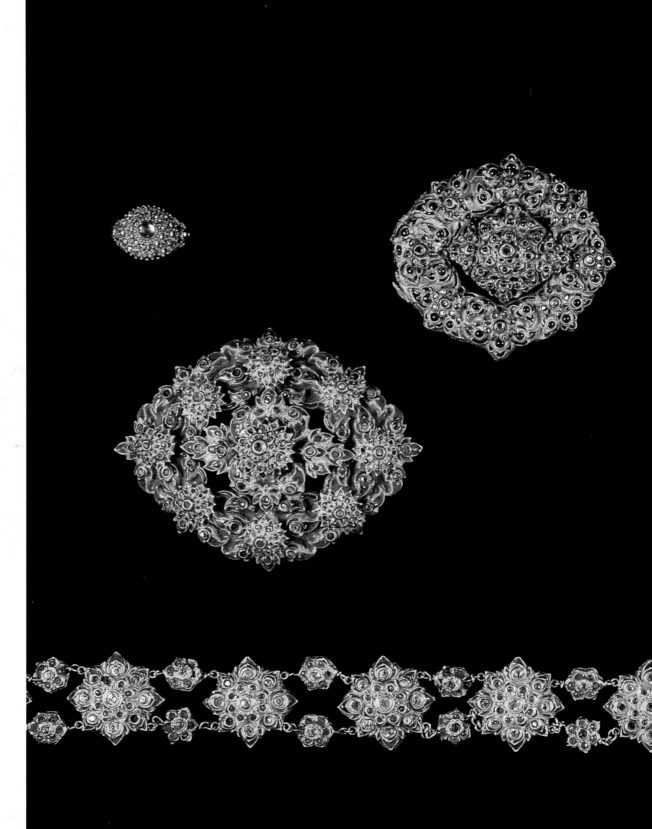

Right: Necklace composed of gold cylinders and beads with attached pendants having a large central gem plus smaller ones and enamelling. Ayutthaya period, *ca* 17th to 18th century. The other pieces comprise gemmed and enamelled jewelry of the Ratanakosin period influenced by Ayutthaya techniques and designs. *Ca* 19th century.

Jewelry, with the exception of pieces from the Ayutthaya National Museum, are courtesy of the collections of Wisarut Buranamanas and Vidhya Dardarananda.

Bibliography

For **The Classic Thai House:**

— Broman, Barry M 1984, *Old Homes of Bangkok*, Bangkok: The Siam Society
— Charernsupkul, Anuvit 1978, *Northern Thai Domestic Architecture and Rituals in House Building*, Bangkok: The Fine Arts Commission of the Association of Siamese Architects
— Charernsupkul, Anuvit 1978, *The Elements of Thai Architecture*, Bangkok: Karm Pim Satri Sarn
— Diskul, Subhadradhis, MC Warren, William Pokakornijan, Oragoon and Baidikul, Viroon 1982, *Suan Pakkad Palace Collection*, Bangkok: Princess Chumbhot of Nagara Savarga
— Jordy, William H 1976, *American Buildings and Their Architects Progressive and Academic Ideals at the Turn of the Twentieth Century*, New York: Anchor Press/Doubleday
— Jumsai, Sumet 1988, *Naga: Cultural Origins in Siam and the West Pacific*, Singapore: Oxford University Press
— Warren, William 1994, *Arts & Crafts in Thailand*, Bangkok: Asia Books Co Ltd
— Warren, William 1985, *Thai Style*, Singapore: Times Editions International
— Warren, William 2001, *The Jim Thompson Collection*, Singapore: Editions Didier Millet

For **Classic Thai Royal and Religious Architecture:**

— Airports Authority of Thailand, 1997, *Chang Sip Mu (Department of the Ten Crafts)*, Bangkok: Amarin Printing and Publishing Public Co, Ltd (in Thai and English)
— Boisselier, Jean 1975 reprinted 1987, *The Heritage of Thai Sculpture*, Bangkok: Asia Books Co Ltd.
— Diskul, Subhadradis MC, Professor, 7th edition 1991, *Art in Thailand a Brief History*, Bangkok: Amarin Printing Group Co Ltd
— Diskul, Subhadradis M.C., Professor (no date). *Sukhothai Art*, Bangkok: The Cultural Committee of The Thailand National Commission for UNESCO. Thai Watana Panich Press Co Ltd
— Electricity Generating Authority of Thailand,1978, *The Grand Palace*, Bangkok: Sirimit Karnpim

— The Fine Arts Department, Division of Archaeology, 1982, *The Sights of Ratanakosin*, Bangkok: Information Section, Office of Secretary, The Fine Arts Department
— Krairiksh, Piriya 1977, *Art Styles in Thailand: A Selection from National Provincial Museums*, Bangkok: The Fine Arts Department
— Krairiksh, Piriya 2001. "The History of Ayutthaya Arts" in *Ayutthaya and Asia*, Charnvit Kasetsiri editor, Bangkok: The Foundation for the Promotion of Social Sciences and Humanities (in Thai and English)
— Listopad, John 1995, *The Art and Architecture of Somdet Phra Narai*, Ph.D. dissertation, University of Michigan, Ann Arbor, unpublished
— Office of Ayutthaya Historic City Project, The Fine Arts Department, 1996, *Ayutthaya Historic City*, Bangkok: Samphan Publishing Co Ltd
— Maitreechitt, Banchob 1999, *The Ubosot of Wat Pho*, Bangkok: The Foundation of the 'Phra Buddha Yod Fa Fund' under His Majesty's Patronage, Amarin Amarin Printing Group Co Ltd (in Thai and English)
— Matic, Kathleen I 1979, *A History of Wat Phra Chetupon and its Buddha Images*. Bangkok: The Siam Society, Thai Watana Panich Press Co Ltd
— Ringis, Rita, coordinator editor 1987, *Treasures from the National Museum Bangkok*, Bangkok: The National Museum Volunteers Group
— Suksri, Naengnoi, 1996 *Palaces of Bangkok*, Bangkok : Asia Books Co Ltd
— Sutthitham, Thada, 1993, *Sukhothai Architecture*, Bangkok: The Fine Arts Department (in Thai with some English captions)

For **Classic Thai Design and Craftsmanship:**

Introduction:
— Higham, Charles and Rachanie Thosarat 1998, *Prehistoric Thailand from Early Settlement to Sukhothai*, Bangkok: River Books
— Hoskin, John 1994, *Buddha Images in the Grand Palace*, Bangkok: The Office of His Majesty's Private Secretary
— Kerr, Rose 1998 reprinted, *Chinese Porcelain of the Qiug Dynasty 1644–1911*, Chicago: Art Media Resources Ltd

Buddha Images:
— Boisselier, Jean 1975, *The Heritage of Thai Sculpture*, New York and Tokyo: Weatherhill
— Griswold, AB 1956, *Dated Buddha Images of Northern Thailand*, Artibus Asiae Supplementum XVI
— Hoskin, John 1994, *Buddha Images in the Grand Palace 1994*, Bangkok: The Office of His Majesty's Private Secretary
— Woodward, Hiram W Jr 1999, *The Sacred Sculpture of Thailand 1999*, The Alexander B. Griswold Collection The Walters Art Gallery, rep. Bangkok: River Books

Ayutthaya Painting:
— Boisselier, Jean 1976, *La Peinture en Thailande*, Fribourg: Office du Livre
— Listopad, John 1995, *The Art and Architecture of Somdet Phra Narai*, Ph.D. dissertation, University of Michigan, Ann Arbor, unpublished
— Leksukhum, Santi 2000, *Temples of Gold: Seven Centuries of Thai Buddhist Paintings*, Bangkok: River Books
— Office of the Prime Minister, 1991, *The Statement of Khun Luang Wat Praduu Song Tham, Royal Evidence* (in Thai)

Ratanakosin Painting:
— Boisselier, Jean 1976, *La Peinture en Thailande*, Fribourg: Office du Livre
— Kanokpongchai, Sangaroon 1982, *Wat Suwannaram*, Bangkok: Muang Boran Publishing House (in Thai and English)
— Suchaxaya, Sudara 1983, *Buddhaisawan Chapel*, Bangkok: Muang Boran Publishing House (in Thai and English)
— The Working Committee for the Publication of Ratanakosin Painting 1982, *Rattanakosin Painting*, Bangkok: Committee for the Ratanakosin Bicentennial Celebration (in Thai and English)

La Na Painting:
— Boisselier, Jean 1976, *La Peinture en Thailande*, Fribourg: Office du Livre
— Simitraong, Sone 1982, *The Structure of Lanna Mural Paintings*, Bangkok: Silpakorn University (Thai)

— Thongmitr, Wiyada 1983, *Wat Phra Singh*, Bangkok: Muang Boran Publishing House (in Thai and English)

Temple Banners:
— Prangwattanakun, Songsak and Patricia Naenna 1990, *Lan Na Textiles*, Bangkok: Amarin Printing Group Co Ltd (in Thai and English)
— Sricharatchanya, Heamakarn 2001, "Wrapped up in the Buddha", *Bangkok Post*, Outlook 5 July, 8.
— Warren, William 1968, *The House on the Khlong*, Tokyo: Privately published

Thai Manuscripts
— National Library, The Fine Arts Deparment 1988, *Thai Lacquer and Gilt Bookcases, Part 2, Vol. III* (Bangkok Period, 191-285), Bangkok (in Thai with some English captions)
— National Library, The Fine Arts Department 1988, *Royal Processions, History and Royal Ceremonies 1988*, Bangkok (in Thai)
— Ginsburg, Henry 2000, *Thai Art and Culture, Historic Manuscripts from Western Collections*, Chiang Mai: Silkworm Books
— Sukphisit, Suthon 1997, *Folk Arts and Folk Culture: The Vanishing Face of Thailand*, Bangkok: Sukphisit Suthon

Textiles:
— Conway, Susan 1992, *Thai Textiles*, Bangkok: Asia Books Co Ltd
— Fraser-Lu, Sylvia 1988, *Handwoven Textiles of South-East Asia*, Singapore: Oxford University Press
— Guy, John 1998, *Woven Cargoes Indian Textiles in the East*, London: Thames and Hudson
— Lefferts, H Leedom, Jr 1992, "Textiles in the Service of Thai Buddhism", Mattiebelle Gittinger and H Leedom Lefferts Jr, *Textiles and the Tai Experience in Southeast Asia*, Washington, DC: The Textile Museum
— Prangwattanakun, Songsak and Patricia Naenna 1990, *Lao Textiles*, Bangkok: Amarin Printing Group Co Ltd (in Thai and English)
— Prangwattanakun, Songsak and Patricia Naenna 1992, *Textiles of Asia: A Common Heritage*, Chiang

Mai: Chiang Mai University, Office of the National Cultural Commission and UNESCO (in English and Thai), 24–39 and Figures 1–27 (in English and Thai)

Thai Furniture:
— Ho Wing Meng, *Straits Furniture*, Singapore: Times Books International
— Handler, Sarah 2002, "The Canopy Bed in the Light of Chinese Architecture", *Orientations*, 23, 1

Scripture Cabinets and Chests:
— Listopad, John 1995, *The Art and Architecture of Somdet Phra Narai*, Ph.D. dissertation, University of Michigan, Ann Arbor, unpublished
— National Library, The Fine Arts Department, 1988, *Thai Lacquer and Gilt Bookcases, Part 2, Vol. III* (Bangkok Period, 191–285), Bangkok (in Thai with some English captions).
— Phanjabhan, Naengnoi and Somchai Na Nakhonphanom 1992, *The Art of Thai Wood Carving, Sukhothai, Ayutthaya, Ratanakosin*, Bangkok: Rerngram Publishing Co Ltd
— Tasukon, Niyadeh 1990, "Foreign Aspects in Decorative Designs on Thai Gilt Lacquered Cabinets", *The Silpakorn Journal 33*, 6 (in Thai and English)

Preaching Chairs:
— Listopad, John 1995, *The Art and Architecture of Somdet Phra Narai*, Ph.D. dissertation, University of Michigan, Ann Arbor, unpublished
— Punjabha, Naengnoi and Somchai Na Nakhonphanom 1992 *The Art of Thai Wood Carving, Sukhothai, Ayutthaya, Ratanakosin*, Bangkok: Rerngrom Publishing Co Ltd

Lan Na Pulpits:
— Punjabhan, Naengnoi, Arun Wichinko and Somcahi Na Nakhonphanom 1994, *The Charm of Lanna Wood Carving*, Bangkok: Rerngram Publishing Co Ltd
— Phanjabhan, Naengnoi and Somchai Na Nakhonphanom 1992, *The Art of Thai Wood Carving, Sukhothai, Ayutthaya, Ratanakosin*, Bangkok: Rerngram Publishing Co Ltd

Ceremonial Containers:
— Punjabhan, Naengnoi 1991, *Silverware in Thailand*, Bangkok: Rerngram Publishing Co Ltd
— The Fine Arts Department 1993 *Thai Minor Arts*, Bangkok: The Fine Arts Department
— Trakullertsathiens, 2001, "Neillo, Neillo", *Bangkok Post*, Outlook 1, 11 October

Gold and Silver Jewelry:
— Brown, Richard S and Maleerat Limsupawnit 2002, *Astral Gemstone Talismans, New Designs 2002*, Bangkok: AGT LTD
— The Fine Arts Department, 1993, *Thai Minor Arts*, Bangkok: The Fine Arts Department
— Punjabhan, Naengnoi 1991, *Silverware in Thailand*, Bangkok: Rerngram Publishing Co Ltd
— Untracht, Oppi 1997, *Traditional Jewelry of India*, London: Thames and Hudson

Ceramics:
— Ayers, John 1980, *Far Eastern Ceramics in the Victoria and Albert Museum*, London: Sotheby Parke Bernet
— Beurdeley, Michel and Guy Raindre 1987, *Qing Porcelain*, London: Thames and Hudson.
— Garner, Harry 1964, *Oriental Blue and White*, London: Faber and Faber Ltd
— Krahl, Regina, John Ayers and Nurdan Erbahar 1986, *Chinese Ceramics in the Topkapi Saray Museum Istanbul, A Complete Catalogue, III*, London: Sotheby's Publications
— Little, Stephen 1984, *Chinese Ceramics of the Transitional Period: 1620–1683*, New York: China Institute in America
— Sjostrand, Sten and Claire Barnes 2002, "The Turiang: A Fourteenth-Century Chinese Shipwreck Upsetting Southeast Asian Ceramic History", *Journal of the Malaysian Branch of the Royal Asiatic Society LXXIV Part 1*, 2001
— Valaikaew, Jaruk 1992, "Cultural Heritage from Under Water, the 'Ao Thai I' junk or the 'Klang-Ao' junk", *Silapakorn Journal*, 35m 2, 8–33 (in Thai and English)

Map of Thailand

MYANMAR (BURMA)

LAOS

VIETNAM

Chiang Rai
Chiang Saen
Phan
Phayao
Chiang Mai
San Kamphaeng
Lamphun
Nan
Lampang
Phrae
VIANGCHAN (Vientiane)
Si Satchanalai
Uttaradit
Sawankhalok
Udon Thani
Nakhon Phanom
Sukhothai
Sakhon Nakhon
Tak (Rahaeng)
Pitsanulok
THAILAND
Kamphaeng Phet
Phichit
Phetchabun
Khon Kaen
Kalasin
Maha Sarakham
Roi Et
Nakornsawan
Chaiyaphum
Suuwannaphum
Ubon Ratchathani
U Thai Thani
Chai Nat
Si Sa Ket
Sing Buri
Lopburi
Nakhon Ratchasima (Khorat)
Buri Ram
Surin
Ang Thong
Suphanburi
Saraburi
Ayutthaya
Kanchanaburi
Nakhon Pathom
Prachinburi
BANGKOK
Thonburi
Samut Prakan
Ratchaburi
Aranyaprathet
CAMBODIA
Chonburi
Petchaburi
Chanthaburi
MYANMAR (BURMA)
PHNOM PENH
Gulf of Thailand (Ao Thai)
VIETNAM
Chumphon
Chaiya
Surat Thani
Andaman Sea
Nakorn Si Thammarat
Krabi
Phuket
Phatthalung
Songkhla
Pattani
Yala
Narathiwat

THAILAND

MALAYSIA

Acknowledgments

It was only possible to produce this book with the kind assistance of many people, to whom we would like to express our deepest appreciation.

In particular, we would like to express our special thanks to interior designer Prinda Puranananda, of the Bangkok design firm Cowperthwaite & Puranananda, who as our interior design consultant contributed hours of her valuable time and helped source many of the houses featured in this book. We owe much of our success to the generous support of Khun Prinda.

We would like to extend our gratitude to the Bangkok National Museum, the National Library, Bangkok, The Prince Rangsit Collection, Rama Art, Bangkok, the Nagi Shop, Bangkok, Neold, Bangkok, the Jim Thompson Collection, Khun Paothong Thongchua , Khun Wisarut Buranamanas and Khun Vidhya Dardarananda, Mr William Booth, Mr Patrick Booth, and Mr Eric Booth for allowing us to borrow and photograph items. Furthermore, many people opened their houses and helped us in other ways. Grateful thanks to M.R. Sukhumbandh Paribatra, Khun Savitree Paribatra, Mr Allan Goodman, Mr Michael Wright, Mr Walter J. Strach III, Mr Eric Booth, M.L. Siriwan Chandaravorachart, Khun Prasan Fargrajang, Mr Gunther Glauninger, Ms Sabine Glauninger, Khun Suchada Bhirom Bhakdi, M.L. Rongrit Pramoj, Khun Neon Snidvongs na Ayudhaya, Khun Pornsri Luphaiboon, Khun Chancham Bunnag, Khun Tew Bunnag, Khun Sorapan Boonpan, Mr Eugene Davis, M.R. Saisanidh Rangsit, Khun Teddy Spha Palasthira, Ms Lan Pajasalmi, Mr Karl Morsbach, Khun Prasart Vongsakul, Khun Anuwat Prompawpan, Mr Richard Engelhardt, Mr David Jacobson, Ms Trina Dingler Ebert and Ms Nina Kumana of Aman Resorts, Ms Kymberley Sproule of the Regent Chiangmai Resort, Mr Christopher Stafford of the Anantara Resort Hua Hin, Mr Bill Bensley of Bensley Design Studios, and Khun Phannee Chirangboonkul of Siphaya International Co Ltd.